THE BIGGEST BOOK OF TALKING BALLS EVER!

First published by Carlton Books in 2016

Carlton Books
20 Mortimer Street
London W1T 3JW

Copyright © Carlton Books 2016

A CIP catalogue for this book is available from the British Library.

ISBN 978-1-78097-876-5

10 9 8 7 6 5 4 3 2 1

Printed and bound by CPI Group (UK) Ltd

THE BIGGEST BOOK OF TALKING BALLS EVER!

Edited by Richard Foster and Adrian Brady

CARLTON
BOOKS

Contents

Introduction

Muhammad Ali, Brian Clough and Geoff Boycott were all at the very top of their game, rightly acknowledged as masters of their sport, but much of their reputation was secured by what they said outside the ring or off the pitch. Their lasting legacy is so much more than just a record of sporting deeds.

Ali floored as many opponents out of the ring as in it. His withering put-downs of George Foreman in particular were as damaging as his lightning-fast hands. My favourite Ali quote sums up his supreme confidence and the cool rationale behind it: "It's not bragging if you can back it up."

Clough was another one skilled in the art of keeping everyone else in his considerable shadow, but he could also be devastatingly funny, as with his comment on Roy Keane's disciplinary problems: "He's had more holidays than Judith Chalmers." Boycott's well-known bluntness is captured in his assessment of English cricket's *enfant terrible* Kevin Pietersen, when he insisted that there were "more brains in a pork pie."

Alongside the sharp, witty put-downs there is also plenty of room in this book for the blunt blunders. So numerous slip-ups and gaffes, which we can all enjoy at others' expense, are featured as well. Despite being an excellent broadcaster, David Coleman will always be remembered for his various cock-ups. His name has become enshrined in popular culture for those notable errors, but he is not alone and there are many tripping over themselves in his wake. Welcome to *The Biggest Book of Talking Balls Ever!*

Richard Foster

Football

As the biggest sport across the globe, football is forever in the spotlight with each wayward word and verbal volley captured. From Arsene to Zlatan, the very best and the worst are featured here.

Football

" He can't kick with his left foot, he can't head, he can't tackle, and he doesn't score that many goals. Apart from that, he's alright. "
George Best on David Beckham

" The average English footballer could not tell the difference between an attractive woman and a corner flag. "
Walter Zenga on English footballers

" Mourinho is the best coach in the world, but as a man he needs to learn manners and respect. "
Mario Balotelli lectures Mourinho on being civil

" In some ways, cramp is worse than having a broken leg. "
Kevin Keegan

" We didn't underestimate them. They were just a lot better than we thought. "
England manager Bobby Robson, after the 1990 World Cup game against Cameroon

" He covers every blade of grass, but that's only because his first touch is crap. "
David Jones on Carlton Palmer

If you expose the opposition's weaknesses enough, then, in the end, those weaknesses will be exposed.
Football manager Sam Allardyce

" Messi can do some amazing things, but anything he can do, Joe Cole can do as well, if not better. "
Steven Gerrard

" I would not be bothered if we lost every game as long as we won the World Cup. "
German footballer Michael Ballack

" Someone said you could write Barry's knowledge of tactics on a stamp. You'd need to fold the stamp in half. "
Steve Claridge on Barry Fry

Football

" And Bale slides the ball inside Cech."
Football commentator John Motson

" You don't need balls to play in a cup final."
Steve Claridge with an anatomical revelation

" Martin O'Neill, standing, hands on hips,
stroking his chin."
BBC sports reporter Mike Ingham

" One accusation you can't throw at me
is that I've always done my best."
Footballer Alan Shearer

" This will be their 19th consecutive game without
a win unless they can get an equalizer."
BBC football commentator Alan Green

He's like my missus – telepathic! Just like her,
he always knew which buttons to press.
Andy Cole on Alex Ferguson

Football

" He's like a second wife. "
**Benni McCarthy on his striking relationship
with Jason Roberts**

" We will wait for him like a good wife waiting
for her husband who is in jail. "
**Jurgen Klopp shows patience with Mats
Hummels' return from injury**

" That David Seaman is a handsome young man
but he spends too much time looking in his
mirror rather than at the ball. "
Brian Clough on David Seaman

" I think Pat's dress sense is dreadful. I would
like to see him in a nice shirt or a proper tie. "
Mary Nevin on son Pat's sartorial sense – or not

" We have a number of two-footed players in this
country at the moment – Morrison, Barkley and
Townsend – and they are unique. "
Just as Jamie Redknapp's many gaffes are unique

" Ed De Goey is the worst-dressed man I've ever seen. One pair of jeans, one pair of trainers, one shirt and one haircut. "
John Terry on teammate and keeper

" You can punch someone, you can go over the top and break someone's leg, which is unnecessary, in a tackle, but to go against team orders in the dressing room is terrible. "
Gary Neville's questionable morality over Kevin Mirallas' penalty miss

" We lost because we didn't win. "
Sweden football manager Lars Lagerback

" I've got nothing against foreign managers, they are very nice people. Apart from Arsene Wenger. "
Tony Pulis getting personal

" To get players to come to Plymouth I had to beat them up and drug them. "
Ian Holloway on unusual recruitment tactics in the South West

> If that had gone in, it would have been a goal.
> **David Coleman**

" If God had wanted us to play football in
the clouds, he'd have put grass up there. "
Brian Clough

" Neil Sullivan has stopped absolutely everything
they have thrown at him… Wimbledon 1,
Manchester United 1. "
Football commentator Mike Ingham

" Sir David Beckham? You're having a laugh. He's
just a good footballer with a famous bird.
Can you imagine if Posh was called Lady
Beckham? We'd never hear the end of it. "
**Ian Holloway on possible knighthood
for Beckham**

" You don't score 64 goals in 86 games
without being able to score goals. "
BBC sports reporter Alan Green

" Every dog has its day, and today is woof day!
Today I just want to bark. "
Ian Holloway's canine take on promotion

" I love Blackpool. We're very similar.
We both look better in the dark. "
Ian Holloway on his affinity with Blackpool

We ended the season on a high – apart
from the last game which we lost.
David Beckham's positive mental attitude

" Everything's been really positive and smooth.
Apart from, obviously, the season. "
**David Beckham taking positive thinking
to a new level at LA Galaxy**

" Mark Hughes at his very best: he loves to feel
people right behind him. "
Kevin Keegan

" I have no doubts whatsoever that Germany will thrash England and qualify easily for the World Cup. What could possibly go wrong? The English haven't beaten us in Munich for 100 years. "
Former German player Uli Hoeness on the eve of Germany's 5-1 defeat to England

" This chance is unmissable and well, er, he misses it! "
Alan Hansen

" If you score against the Italians you deserve a goal. "
Ron Atkinson

" I'm not saying we shouldn't have a foreign manager, but I think he should definitely be English. "
Paul Merson making the case for an English-speaking manager

" I feel I have broken the ice with the English people. In 60 days, I have gone from being Volvo Man to Svensational. "
Sven-Goran Eriksson

" The ageless Dennis Wise, now in his 30s. "
Football commentator Martin Tyler

" Gotze's leaving because he's Guardiola's favourite. If it's anyone's fault, it's mine. I can't make myself shorter and learn Spanish. "
Jurgen Klopp takes Mario Gotze's departure to Bayern Munich personally

" Thank you to the mothers who gave birth to these Atleti players… their sons have massive balls. "
Diego Simeone is clearly a mummy's boy, after they beat Chelsea in Champions League semi-final

" Romario punched me in the face from behind. You know what? I deserved it. "
Diego Simeone's brutal honesty

" So, Romelu Lukaku, you speak six languages. Which ones? Obviously, there's Belgian… "
Commentator Pat Murphy fails even to get one out of the six as, in Lukaku's Belgian homeland, the languages are Flemish and French

" He dribbles a lot and opposition doesn't like it
– you can see it all over their faces."
Ron Atkinson

" I'd love to be a mole on the wall in the
Liverpool dressing room at half-time."
Kevin Keegan

" We haven't had the rub of the dice."
Bobby Robson

" If someone comes in with a mobile phone, I'll
throw it in the North Sea. And we need lectures
about why we can't have everyday things like
mayonnaise, ketchup and Coke."
Paolo Di Canio sets down some rules

I saw him in the tunnel and thought "Christ,
it's Jack and the Beanstalk, this!"
Alex Bruce sizing up Peter Crouch

" Footballers are no different from human beings. "
Former England manager Graham Taylor

" McCarthy shakes his head in agreement
with the referee. "
Football commentator Martin Tyler

One thing's for sure, a World Cup without
me is nothing to watch.
**Zlatan Ibrahimovic on the global
disappointment over Sweden's failure to qualify**

" You can never beat Alex Ferguson and when
you do you come off second best. "
**Steve McClaren, Fergie's Number Two,
knows his place**

" It's the end-of-season curtain-raiser. "
Former Aston Villa striker Peter Withe

" It's getting tickly now – squeaky-bum time, I call it. "
Sir Alex Ferguson on feeling the pressure of a tight title race

" I'd like to have seen Tony Morley left on as a down-and-out winger. "
Blackpool legend and football commentator Jimmy Armfield

" Anybody who is thinking of applying for the Scotland job in the next eight or nine years should go get themselves checked out by about 15 psychiatrists. "
Martin O'Neill airs his views on head coach

So I'm a liar? He's thin then, that gives reason to call me a liar.
Marco Materazzi lays it on thick in a spat with Rafa Benitez

" I have watched Barnsley and it is clear they are not Real Madrid."
Roberto Mancini is clearly on his game

" Probably when Lionel Messi ran straight past me."
David Beckham on realizing it was time to retire

" What do you think they're smoking over there at The Emirates?"
Liverpool owner JW Henry is disparaging about an Arsenal bid for Luis Suarez

" ...and their manager, Terry Neill, isn't here today, which suggests he is elsewhere."
Football commentator Brian Moore

I'm not going to make it a target but it is something to aim for.
Ex-Manchester United star Steve Coppell

Football

" Jose was one of those guys on a surfboard who could stay longer on the wave than anyone else. "
Alex Ferguson on surfer Mourinho

" Money isn't the most important thing. It is important, of course. I am not Mahatma Gandhi. "
Jurgen Klopp on materialism

" Real possession football this. And Zico's lost it. "
Football commentator John Helm

" Queen's Park against Forfar – you can't get more romantic than that. "
Archie McPherson

" It's a game of two teams. "
BBC football reporter Peter Brackley

" We were not good enough today, particularly in the fringe department. "
Sam Allardyce gives his team a hair-dressing down

" Well, we got nine and you can't score more
than that. "
**Former England football manager
Bobby Robson**

" Maybe Louis does have a golden willy. "
Arjen Robben on van Gaal's magic touch

" It was like something out of *Swan Lake*
– it's that blatant. "
Steve Bruce on Gary Cahill's balletic dive

" He's worse than Dracula, because at least
Dracula comes out of his coffin now
and then. "
**Bruce Grobbelaar gets his teeth
into Simon Mignolet**

" Manchester City have got the best, if not the
second-best, squad in the league. "
Georgie Bingham just cannot make up her mind

Football

" I am a firm believer that if you score one goal the other team have to score two to win. "
Howard Wilkinson

" Football's a game of skill; we kicked them a bit and they kicked us a bit. "
**Former England football hard man
Graham Roberts**

Sometimes you want Obertan to open his legs and do something a bit exciting.
Alan Pardew

" Mario Balotelli is like Marmite, you either love him or hate him. Me, I'm in between. "
Joe Royle

" White liquid in a bottle has to be milk. "
Rafa Benitez

Football

" More chuffed than a badger at the start
of the mating season. "
**Ian Holloway expresses his joy
in black and white**

" For all his horses, knighthoods, or
championships, he hasn't got two of what
I've got. And I don't mean balls. "
**Brian Clough on the difference between
himself and Alex Ferguson before he won his
second Champions League trophy**

" There's a one-man Liverpool wall, hurriedly
put together. "
Football commentator John Murray

There are a whole lot of teams in the
bottom six this season.
Graeme Le Saux

" We had already beaten them 4-0 and 7-0 earlier
this season, so we knew we were in for a really
tough game today."
**Barry Ferguson never underestimates his
opponents**

" Viv Anderson has pissed a fatness test."
John Helm aka Mrs Malaprop

" Maths is totally done differently to what
I was teached when I was at school."
David Beckham

I'd love the person who taught Jose Mourinho
English to taught me.
So do we Steve Claridge, so do we

" With Harry [Redknapp], two plus two makes five,
not three."
Milan Mandaric sums it up

Football

" Argentina won't be at Euro 2000 because
they are from South America. "
**Kevin Keegan's logic is as strong as his
geography**

" Football's like a big market place and people go to
the market every day to buy their vegetables. "
Bobby Robson's low opinion of footballers

" Chris Waddle is off the pitch at the moment –
exactly the position he is at his most menacing. "
Gerald Sinstadt

" I'd like to think it's a case of crossing the
i's and dotting the t's. "
Former manager Dave Bassett

" I never predict anything and I never will do. "
Footballer Paul Gascoigne

" These are players that are trying to put food
in the manager's head. "
Ex-player Jason McAteer gives food for thought

" If someone in the crowd spits at you, you have just
got to swallow it. "
Gary Lineker

" We'll not give up even if we're 12 points behind
with one game left. "
**Joe Hart, whose spirit is stronger
than his maths**

If you just need a first eleven and four others, why
did Columbus sail to India to discover America?
**Claudio Ranieri poses the question we all
want to know**

" Kicked wide of the goal with such precision. "
Football presenter Des Lynam

" They're the second-best team in the world
and there's no higher praise than that. "
Kevin Keegan

Football

" Chips without mayonnaise is not chips. "
Ronald Koeman

" We have to score more goals than we concede
to win a game of football. "
Sam Allardyce, master tactician

" I'm not going to pick out anyone in particular,
but Jay-Jay Okocha should not be captain of a
football club. "
Former footballer Rodney Marsh

" I saw him kick the bucket over there, which
suggests he's not going to be able to continue. "
Football pundit Trevor Brooking

" That's football, Mike. Northern Ireland have had
several chances and haven't scored but England
had no chances and scored twice. "
Trevor Brooking

" I'm going to make a prediction; it could
go either way. "
Ron Atkinson sitting on the fence

" Goodnight, and don't forget to put your cocks back."
Football pundit Jimmy Hill

" And there's Ray Clemence looking as cool as ever out in the cold."
Jimmy Hill

I've told the players we need to win so that I can have the cash to buy some new ones.
Football manager Chris Turner

" Money has never won anything."
Profound from Petr Cech – and maybe hypocritical

" How can you replace Fergie's record? You could live to be one million years old and not see it surpassed."
Tommy Docherty goes long on longevity

Football

" I've eaten a bar of soap before and then
I swear like a trooper. "
Ian Holloway cleans up his act

" He had an eternity to play that ball…
but he took too long over it. "
Football commentator Martin Tyler

" I'm very excited to see him in the flesh
and play with him. "
**Theo Walcott may be getting too
excited about Ozil's arrival**

" If you want, you can make a silence very noisy.
You could make noise with my silence. "
The enigmatic Jose Mourinho

I never comment on referees and I'm not going
to break the habit of a lifetime for that prat.
Ron Atkinson

Football

" Peter Reid is hobbling, and I've got a feeling that will slow him down. "
Football commentator John Motson

" The weather was good, everything was great. Only the result was shit. "
Jurgen Klopp on 2013 Champions League Final

" Last year I ate beef, now I have chicken but I'm still really hungry. "
David Luiz on his appetite for more titles

" It's a lovely ice cream that has been melting in the sun for the last 16 months. "
Guillem Balague sums up Barcelona's humbling defeat to Bayern Munich

" The new West Stand casts a giant shadow over the entire pitch, even on a sunny day. "
Chris Jones seems in the dark

Football

" I've never had a big head. I do not consider
myself to be the best in the world, nor the worst.
I am me and that is enough. "
Mario Balotelli

" I've got a plan to stop him, it's called
a machete. Plan B is a machine gun! "
**Sir Alex Ferguson on how to
counter Ronaldo**

" I'll probably open a bottle of champagne tonight…
I might even treat myself to a bag of crisps. "
Neil Warnock

" I was recognised too much and sometimes
women would suddenly climb all over me. "
Marouane Fellaini

Sergio Ramos is a fantastic football player,
but he is not a doctor.
Jose Mourinho

Football

" You've got to miss them to score sometimes. "
Football manager Dave Bassett

Unfortunately, we keep kicking ourselves in the foot.
Ray Wilkins

" The most vulnerable area for goalies is between their legs... "
Football commentator Andy Gray

" Brazil – they're so good it's like they are running around the pitch playing with themselves. "
Football commentator John Motson

" Coaches are like watermelons. "
Massimo Cellino

I use the word embarrassing because I'm trying to be respectful.
Gus Poyet after 8-0 defeat to Southampton

" Alex McLeish and I even competed for the acne cream when we were younger. Obviously, I won that one. "
Gordon Strachan is spot on

" I tried to get the disappointment out of my system by going for a walk. I ended up 17 miles from home and I had to phone my wife Lesley to come and pick me up. "
Gordon Strachan

" If that was a penalty, we should be playing basketball. "
Niko Kovac, Croatian manager

" He was old a year ago, now he's young. "
Gary Neville on Ryan Giggs, aka Peter Pan

" The best way to win games is to score goals. "
Manuel Pellegrini on tactical nuances

" It's like having a choice between two blokes
to nick your wife. "
Gary Neville's take on Hobson's choice

" If history is going to repeat itself I should
think we can expect the same thing again. "
Terry Venables

" I'm not a believer in luck... but I do believe
you need it. "
Former England footballer Alan Ball

" If that ball had dropped to a West Brom
player who'd put it in the net, that would
have been the equalizer. "
**Trevor Francis should know as
he was a lethal striker in his playing days**

" Congratulations to him, he's got the chance to wave his fingers at a few more managers in this competition."
Tim Sherwood on Benfica boss Jorge Jesus

The lad got overexcited when he saw the whites of the goalpost's eyes.
Steve Coppell

" Newcastle, of course, unbeaten in their last five wins."
Brian Moore

" They are men. I'm a manager, not a babysitter."
Tim Sherwood – not keen on his own players either

" Some people are frustrated with that result? Some people can **** off."
Mick McCarthy

" This is football from the 19th century. The
only thing I can bring more to win was a
Black & Decker to destroy the wall. "
**Jose Mourinho on West Ham United's
Victorian approach**

I couldn't give a ****. Good old Jose,
moaning again.
**Sam Allardyce, unimpressed by
Mourinho's 19th century dig**

" It's not helpful when the three fountains
of knowledge on *Match of the Day* make a
mountain out of a molehill. "
Nigel Pearson

" My parents have been there for me,
ever since I was about seven. "
David Beckham

" He was a quiet man, Eric Cantona, but
he was a man of few words. "
David Beckham

I said to my players I was squeezing my ass but it was
the wrong expression. I have twitched my ass on the
bench because we were out of balance.
Louis van Gaal

" Football's not just physical, it's menthol too. "
Football manager Phil Brown

" Benitez took the elephant in the room
and put it on the table. "
Gareth Southgate

" I don't want Rooney to leave these shores
but if he does, I think he'll go abroad. "
Ian Wright

" Stokes gets a straight yellow for that challenge. "
Ronnie Whelan

" Arsenal literally finished the game after
15 minutes. "
Former Arsenal striker Ian Wright

" If you don't give Martinez a chance,
what chance has he got? "
Paul Merson

" I've served more time than Ronnie Biggs
did for the Great Train Robbery. "
Malcolm Allison on a touchline ban

Liverpool will be without Kvarme tonight
– he's illegible.
Jimmy Armfield

" Devon Loch was a better finisher."
Ron Atkinson on Carlton Palmer

Great teams always have a Plan B. Look at Barcelona. Their Plan B is to stick to Plan A.
Pundit Johnny Giles

Jimmy Hill: Don't sit on the fence, Terry, what chance do you think Germany has got of getting through?
Terry Venables: I think it's 50-50.

" There's nobody fitter at his age, except maybe Raquel Welch."
Ron Atkinson on 39-year-old Gordon Strachan

" It's nice for us to have a fresh face in the camp to bounce things off."
Lawrie Sanchez

" They didn't change positions, they just moved the players around. "
Terry Venables

" I know where the linesman should've stuck his flag, and he would have had plenty of help. "
Ron Atkinson

" If that was a penalty I'll plait sawdust. "
Ron Atkinson

The Sheffield United strip looks as if it was designed by Julian Clary when he had a migraine.
Sean Bean

" I used to go missing a lot – Miss Canada, Miss United Kingdom, Miss Germany. "
George Best

" Liverpool are my nap selection – I prefer to sleep when they're on the box. "
Stan Bowles

" Michael Owen – he's got the legs of a salmon. "
Craig Brown

" If Glenn Hoddle said one word to his team at half-time, it was concentration and focus. "
Ron Atkinson

" I think that was a moment of cool panic there. "
Ron Atkinson

I would not say he [David Ginola] is the best left winger in the Premiership, but there are none better.
Ron Atkinson

This is the first time Denmark has ever reached the World Cup Finals, so this is the most significant moment in Danish history.
Football commentator John Helm

" And I honestly believe we can go all the way to Wembley – unless somebody knocks us out. "
Dave Bassett

" At Rangers I was third choice left back – behind an amputee and a Catholic. "
Craig Brown

" Footballers' wives should be seen and not heard. "
Tony Waiters

" This is an unusual Scotland side because they have good players. "
Javier Clemente, Spanish coach

Football

" He's had more holidays than Judith Chalmers. "
**Brian Clough on Roy Keane's long line
of suspensions**

" Ally MacLeod thinks tactics are a new kind of
mint. "
Billy Connolly

" Atillio Lombardo is starting to pick up a bit of
English on the training ground. The first word
he learned was 'wanker'. "
Steve Coppell

" I felt sorry for the match ball – it came off the
pitch crying. "
Johann Cruyff

Doug Ellis said he was right behind me. I told
him I'd sooner have him in front of me where
I could see him.
Tommy Docherty

" Most people who can remember when (Notts) County were a great club are dead."
Jack Dunnett

" One Wigan director wanted us to sign Salford Van Hire because he thought he was a Dutch international."
Fred Eyre

" Nicky Butt's a real Manchester boy. He comes from Gorton, where it is said they take the pavements in of a night time."
Alex Ferguson

I still believe we have an outside chance of reaching the Play-Offs, but then again, I believe in Father Christmas.
Trevor Francis

" I was delighted to get a point. Normally the only thing we get out of London is the train from Euston. "
Jimmy Frizzell, Oldham manager

Hugo Sanchez is a very dangerous man. He is about as welcome as a piranha in a bidet.
Jesus Gil

" The first thing I read now in the *Telegraph* is the obituaries. If I'm not in it, I have a good day. "
Jack Hayward

" We are down to the barest knuckle. "
Glenn Hoddle

" The biggest problem I've got down here in Plymouth is seagulls shitting on my car. "
Ian Holloway

Football

" Only God knows …You're talking to him now. "
Zlatan Ibrahimovic

" Ian Rush unleashed his left foot and it hit
the back of the net. "
Mike England

" Wilkins sends an inch-perfect pass to no
one in particular. "
Bryon Butler

" The World Cup – truly an international event. "
Football commentator John Motson

" If you can't stand the heat in the dressing room,
get out of the kitchen. "
Terry Venables

For those of you watching in black and white,
Spurs are playing in yellow.
Football commentator John Motson

Football

" I sent myself off. It's impossible to be more embarrassed than that. There was nothing more I could do so I went to the dressing room."
Phil Scolari's novel way of dealing with defeat at Gremio

When I sleep too much I don't score. That's the reason I go out a lot.
Romario on his unusual training regime

" Neymar is the Justin Bieber of football. Brilliant on the old YouTube. Cat piss in reality."
Joey Barton

" It was like seducing the most beautiful woman in the world. Then failing on the moment for which you did it all."
Socrates on the disappointment of Brazil's 1982 World Cup exit

Football

" Some people tell me that we professional players are slaves. Well, if this is slavery, give me a life sentence. "
Bobby Charlton

" Playing against a defensive opposition is just as bad as making love to a tree. "
Jorge Valdano

" It was a game of two halves and we were rubbish in both of them. "
Brian Horton

" His weakness is that he doesn't think he has any. "
Arsene Wenger on Alex Ferguson

The highest educated person at Real Madrid is the woman cleaning the toilets.
Joan Gaspart, Barcelona president

" There are only three things that stand still in the air: a hummingbird, a helicopter and Dada."
Brazilian footballer Dada Maravilha

Those who tell you it's tough at the top have never been at the bottom.
Joe Harvey

" I know more about football than politics."
Harold Wilson

" If Stan Bowles could pass a betting shop like he can pass a ball he'd have no worries at all."
Ernie Tagg, Crewe manager

" Both teams were feeling each other in the first half."
John Terry goes a bit tactile over Chelsea's match against PSG

Football

" I tell you what, that's a great tackle... Actually
it's a foul, no doubt about it. I can't believe
the ref has let him get away with that."
Robbie Savage proving he can argue with himself

" I can't help but laugh at how perfect I am."
Zlatan Ibrahimovic

" Belgium is not a hotpot of international football."
Alan Brazil

They gave the Serbian FA a poultry fine.
**Alan Brazil feels the authorities are a
little bit chicken**

" Some players need a boot up the backside. Other
players need the arm."
Alan Brazil

> It's real end-to-end stuff, but unfortunately it's all up at Forest's end.
> **Chris Kamara gets a bit dizzy**

" Statistics are there to be broken."
Chris Kamara

" Manchester City are defending like beavers."
Chris Kamara

" If you're chopping and changing the team you don't get that word I can't pronounce beginning with 'C'."
Paul Merson

" People just looked lost. Too many players looked like fish on trees."
Paul Merson

" I'm feeling a lot of pressure with the swan in Scotland. It's not far and I'm more scared of the swan than of football. What's football compared to life? A swan with bird flu, for me that's a drama. "
Jose Mourinho on bird flu

" If the club decide to sack me because of bad results that's part of the game. If it happens I will be a millionaire and get another club a couple of months later. "
Jose Mourinho does not seem too worried

If Chelsea are naïve and pure then I'm Little Red Riding Hood.
Rafa Benitez's fairy tale

" He makes you feel 25-foot tall and I'm going to sorely miss him. "
Ian Holloway on Mourinho being sacked by Chelsea

Football

" I've been consistent in patches this season. "
Theo Walcott

" It was goalposts for jumpers. "
Tony Mowbray mixing up his analogy

I think one of these teams could win this.
**Andy Townsend accurately predicts UEFA
Super Cup Final**

" Javier Pastore wouldn't get a beach ball off
me if we were locked in a phone box. "
Joey Barton

" I can't protect people who don't want to run and
train, and are about three stone overweight. "
**Harry Redknapp not being very protective of
Adel Taarabt**

" If you don't know the answer to that question then I think you are an ostrich. Your head must be in the sand. "
Nigel Pearson in a spat with Ian Baker, a local journalist

" What Carew does with a football, I can do with an orange. "
Zlatan Ibrahimovic

" You bought a Ferrari but you drive it like a Fiat. "
Ibrahimovic on his career at Barcelona

Frank Lampard has still got the same legs he had five years ago.
No leg transplants for the Chelsea man as far as coach Ray Wilkins can see

I like fireworks too, but I set them off in gardens or kebab stands. I never set fire to my own house.
Ibrahimovic distances himself from Mario Balotelli

" I managed lots of clubs. I had more clubs than Jack Nicholson. "
Bobby Gould

" Aaron Ramsey hasn't always been the flavour of the Arsenal fans' eyes. "
Craig Burley

" It can only happen in football – it's the Rocky Balboa scenario. "
Alvin Martin

" It's a real day for Nigel Adkins today, really. "
Martin Keown gets real

Football

" Whatever happened to Dagenham and Redgrave? "
Alan Brazil

" What I saw in Holland and Germany was
that the majority of people are Dutch in Holland
and German in Germany. "
Peter Taylor on Europe

Manchester City are built on sand and I don't
mean that because their owners are from the Arab
countries.
Kevin Keegan

" The aura of uninvincibility has gone,
if there is such a word. "
Adrian Chiles

" I can see the carrot at the end of the tunnel. "
Stuart Pearce on his unusual vision

Football

" I'd like to play for an Italian club, like Barcelona. "
Mark Draper

" Running is for animals. You need a brain and a
ball for football. "
Louis van Gaal

" Van Gaal is a dictator, with no sense of humour. "
Ibrahimovic

" It was nice to hear Ray Wilkins speaking
so articulate. "
Micky Quinn

" I've watched the replay and there is absolutely
no doubt: it's inconclusive. "
Garth Crooks

" Hopefully Andy (Carroll) has only tweeted
his hamstring. "
Sam Allardyce

" Have Liverpool done too much tinkering and tailoring with their system?"
Stan Collymore

At Chelsea, a sacking is just another day at the office.
Andre Villas-Boas

" I like Balotelli: he's even crazier than me. He can score a winner, then set fire to the hotel."
Ibrahimovic praises Balotelli

" The minute's silence was immaculate, I have never heard a minute's silence like that."
Glenn Hoddle

" The world looks a totally different place after two wins. I can even enjoy watching *Blind Date* or laugh at *Noel's House Party*."
Gordon Strachan

I was surprised, but I always say nothing surprises me in football.
Les Ferdinand

" One or two bad eggs have spoiled it. If it had been done my way, they would have been out of the building straight away. "
Joey Barton

" A football team is like a piano. You need eight men to carry it and three who can play the damn thing. "
Bill Shankly

" There was nothing wrong with the timing, he was just a bit late. "
Mark Bright

" A boy from Croxteth should not use hair product. "
Jamie Carragher on Wayne Rooney

Football

" All I really want is for Crystal Palace to win every game between now and the end of time. "
Eddie Izzard on becoming a director of the club

" Someone in the England team will have to grab the ball by the horns. "
Doesn't TV football pundit and former manager Ron Atkinson know about the handball rule?

" I've told you a million times, I don't exaggerate. "
Former Arsenal striker Charlie Nicholas

Nethercott is literally standing in Le Tissier's pocket.
BBC pundit David Pleat sees some strange things in an English football match

Football

" Sporting Lisbon in their green and white hoops,
looking like a team of zebras. "
**Clearly BBC sports reporter Peter Jones
hasn't been to the zoo lately**

" Forest have now lost six matches
without winning. "
David Coleman

" Goalkeepers aren't born today
until they're in their late 20s or 30s. "
**That's some gestation period according
to former player and manager Kevin Keegan**

" Aston Villa have literally metaphorically had their
pants pulled down. "
Dion Dublin talking total pants

Gary always weighed up his options,
especially when he had no choice.
Kevin Keegan

" You can see the ball go past them, or the man,
but you'll never see both man and ball go past
at the same time. So if the ball goes past, the
man won't, or if the man goes past, they'll
take the ball. "
Ron Atkinson... and his point was?

Fulham needed that three points because they
were slowly sinking to the bottom of the table
very, very quickly.
Pundit Mark Lawrenson is no judge of speed

" He's been one of the best centre backs/full backs
for the past 12 decades. "
**Liverpool's Jamie Carragher has had a
very long-playing career according to
fellow player Michael Owen**

" Brooking trying one of those impossible crosses,
which on that occasion was impossible. "
Brian Moore

When Paul Scholes gets it [tackling] wrong,
they come in so late that they arrive yesterday.
Time travel for Ron Atkinson

" Emile Zola has scored again for Chelsea. "
**A BBC Radio 5 Live commentator
sees the literary side of a football match**

" It's now 1–1, an exact reversal of the score
line on Saturday. "
Radio 5 Live

" The Uruguayans are losing no time in
making a meal around the referee. "
This match was no picnic for Mike Ingham

" Poland 0, England 0, though England are
now looking the better value for their nil. "
**Nil points for the logic of BBC
sports commentator Barry Davies**

Football

" Arsenal shouldn't be too concerned, because every team has a bit of a blip during the season. Last year they had one. "
Football's Ray Wilkins

" I would advise anyone coming to the match to come early and not to leave until the end, otherwise they might miss something. "
Football pundit John Toshack

Peru score their third, and it's 3-1 to Scotland. **There's that old maths problem again for David Coleman**

" Ian Rush is deadly 10 times out of 10, but that wasn't one of them. "
3 out of 10 on commentary for Peter Jones

Football

And there'll be more football in a moment, but first we've got the highlights of the Scottish League Cup Final.
BBC sports reporter Gary Newbon

" Petr Cech will want a clean sheet having been unusually leaky in the past few weeks. "
Match of the Day **commentator gets personal about the Chelsea goalkeeper**

" After that (the Simon Davies goal), you just could smell it – Hamburg got very nervous. "
Summarizer Chris Coleman can sniff out a victory

" Julian Dicks is everywhere. It's like they've got eleven Dicks on the field. "
Britain's Metro Radio commentator makes a dick of himself

Football

" For me their biggest threat is when they
get into the attacking part of the field. "
Ron Atkinson gets down to the ethos of football

" Football's football: if that weren't the
case it wouldn't be the game that it is. "
So said the BBC's Garth Crooks

" Steven Gerrard makes runs into the box
better than anyone. So does Frank Lampard. "
**Former Premier League player and
commentator Jamie Redknapp**

Sometimes in football you have to score goals.
**Even if you resort to using your hands, according
to French footballer Thierry Henry**

Football

" Portuguese international singer Cristiano Ronaldo has signed a two-year extension to his contract. "
The CNN online football report announces a change of career for the player

" I would love to be able to get to the stage where things are all rosy in the garden. But I am not yet looking at pastures new, although right now we have given the critics a field day. "
Football manager Alex McLeish gets all horticultural

" Henchoz advanced to the halfway line and exposed himself. "
Former footballer and summarizer Graeme Le Saux was on to that in a flash

" Well, Real Madrid might have got the points, but it was an unconvincing 1-0 draw. "
Sky Sport's Rob Palmer makes it far from clear

" I always want to play for my country.
I'm here if they need me for the rest of
my life, and hopefully after that as well. "
**Brazil's Romario is in heaven about
playing for the national side**

" It's difficult to find a defect on Mourinho, perhaps
he is a little introverted but he is marvellous. "
**Inter Milan president Massimo Moratti
is none too sure about coach Jose Mourinho!**

" West Germany's Briegel hasn't been able
to get past anyone yet – that's his trademark. "
BBC sports reporter John Helm

It's headed away by John Clark, using his head.
**Football commentator Derek Rae clearly
wasn't using his, though**

Football

" And with just four minutes gone,
the score is already 0–0. "
**Impressive deduction from
BBC sports reporter Ian Darke**

The USA are a goal down, and if
they don't get a goal they'll lose.
John Helm

" Celtic manager Davie Hay still has
a fresh pair of legs up his sleeve. "
Football pundit John Greig

" At half-time Ardiles said go out there
and throw the kitchen sink at them.
Spurs are doing that, literally. "
**Doesn't former footballer Alan Mullery know
that sink throwing is a red-card offence?**

" It was the game that put the Everton ship
back on the road. "
BBC sports reporter Alan Green

" I couldn't settle in Italy – it was like
living in a foreign country. "
**Liverpool legend Ian Rush on his
spell at Juventus**

" I want to win the Nobel Peace Prize – and I'm
going to fight as hard as I can to make it happen. "
Brazil football star Ronaldo

It falls to the ageless 35-year-old Frank Lampard.
**Does George Hamilton think
Lampard is Methuselah?**

Even when you're dead you shouldn't lie
down and let yourself be buried.
Football manager Gordon Lee

" The Spaniards have been reduced to aiming
aimless balls into the box. "
Ron Atkinson

" A few question marks are being asked
of the Honduran defence. "
Alan Green

" I think if they hadn't scored, we might
have got a better result. "
**Former Leeds United manager
Howard Wilkinson**

" He's got his hands on his knees and holds
his head in despair. "
Peter Jones

" The last player to score a hat-trick in a cup final was Stan Mortenson. He even had a final named after him – the Matthews final. "
Football history is not a strong point for former manager Lawrie McMenemy

" If you stand still there is only one way to go, and that's backwards. "
England goalkeeping legend Peter Shilton

" I had a lump in my mouth as the ball went in. "
Former England manager Terry Venables

" Wenger is still sweating on Sol Campbell's hamstring. "
Is Arsenal's website giving away medical secrets?

Some of these players never dreamed they'd be playing in a cup final at Wembley – but here they are today, fulfilling those dreams.
Lawrie McMenemy

And Ritchie has now scored 11 goals, exactly double the number he scored last season.
BBC sports reporter Alan Parry

" So different from the scenes in 1872, at the FA Cup that none of us can remember."
BBC football commentator John Motson

" They can beat anybody on the day, but they can also lose against anybody on the day."
Former Liverpool football star Emlyn Hughes

" With the last kick of the game,
Bobby McDonald scored with a header."
Alan Parry

" Sessegnon gets it on his left-hand foot."
Is Iain Dowie watching handball or football?

Football

" If you're 0–0 down, there's no one
better to get you back on terms than
Michael Owen. "
**Former player and match summarizer
Andy Townsend**

" A run of 24 games without defeat must be
a millstone on your shoulders. "
**Reverse thinking here from the BBC's
Tony Gubba**

" I want more from David Beckham.
I want him to improve on perfection. "
**Kevin Keegan was quite demanding
as England football manager**

Marseille needed to score first, and that never looked
likely once Liverpool had taken the lead.
David Pleat

" You can't do better than go away from
home and get a draw. "
**Kevin Keegan reckons without the
possibility of a win**

Well, let's say there's no place like Wembley
for the winners and there certainly isn't for
the runners-up.
BBC commentator

" Hamburg are the European champions! "
**ITV football commentator Brian Moore
immediately after the final whistle of
the 1980 European Cup final, which
Nottingham Forest had won 1–0**

" He's shown a lack of inconsistency. "
**Former Premier League
manager Chris Coleman**

Interviewer: "Teko, what's your favourite food?"
Teko: "It's hard, but I'm going to have
to say breakfast."
Orlando Pirates midfielder Teko Modise

" If ever a goal ever needed a game, this is it. "
Former footballer Tony Gale

" Fire and broomstick. "
Football pundit David O'Leary

" Well, I've seen some tackles, Jonathan,
but that was the ultimatum! "
Alan Mullery

" Jurgen Klinsmann, who refutes
to earn £25,000 a week... "
**Alan Mullery reckons Klinsmann is in denial
about his pay deal**

He's not going to adhere himself to the fans.
Another malapropism from Alan Mullery

" It doesn't endow me, to be honest. "
Alan Mullery

" I can't understand the notoriety of people. "
Alan Mullery

Alan Brazil: Will he be doing any commentaries for us during the World Cup?
Co-commentator: Well not unless he's going to be doing them from the grave, Alan.

" Our talking point this morning is George Best, his liver transplant and the booze culture in football. Don't forget, the best caller wins a crate of John Smith's. "
Alan Brazil

Football

" Our central defenders, Doherty and Anthony Gardner, were fantastic and I told them that when they go to bed tonight they should think of each other. "
David Pleat

" Never go for a 50-50 ball unless you are 80-20 sure. "
BBC football correspondent Ian Darke

The man [Sir Alex Ferguson] is United through and through – cut him and he bleeds red.
So presumably would Alan Brazil, too

" If we played like that every week we wouldn't be so inconsistent. "
Former Manchester United player Bryan Robson

Football

" It's hard to be passionate twice a week. "
George Graham on Arsenal's
punishing schedule

" The Arsenal defence is skating close
to the wind. "
Obviously a cold wind for football
pundit Jack Charlton

" And sitting on the Watford bench is Ernie
Whalley's brother Tom. Both Welshmen. "
Brian Moore

" They've flown in from all over the world,
so have the rest of the world team. "
Brian Moore

Bryon Butler: "Did you ever have any doubts
about yourself when you left Tottenham?"
Peter Shreeve: "I don't think so."

" Celtic were at one time nine points ahead, but somewhere along the road, their ship went off the rails. "
Football reporter Richard Park seems all at sea

" That's Robson – a total convicted player. "
Jimmy Armfield

If we get promotion, let's sit down and see where we stand.
Football manager Roy McFarland

" Sir Alex is going to continue to keep going. "
Tautology from Manchester United's Gary Neville

" Nearly all the Brazilian supporters are wearing yellow shirts – it's a fabulous kaleidoscope of colour! "
Colour is not John Motson's strong point

" I don't know why Glenn Murray took the penalty. I suppose because he is our penalty taker. "
Brighton Albion manager Gus Poyet

" Paul Gascoigne has recently become a father and been booked for over-celebrating. "
John Motson

That's an old Ipswich move – O'Callaghan crossing for Mariner to drive over the bar.
John Motson

" An inch or two either side of the post and that would have been a goal. "
Dave Bassett speaking on Sky Sports

" Both sides have scored a couple of goals, and both sides have conceded a couple of goals. "
Peter Withe, speaking on Radio 5 Live

...but Arsenal are quick to credit Bergkamp with laying on 75 per cent of their nine goals.
Tony Gubba

" Beckenbauer really has gambled all his eggs."
Ron Atkinson

" We threw our dice into the ring and turned up trumps."
Pundit Bruce Rioch reckons football's a gamble

...and the news from Guadalajara, where the temperature is 96 degrees, is that Falcao is warming up.
Brian Moore

" I spent four indifferent years at Goodison Park,
but they were great years. "
Former goalkeeper Martin Hodge

Souness gave Fleck a second chance and
he grabbed it with both feet.
Journalist James Sanderson

" They have missed so many chances they
must be wringing their heads in shame. "
Former England manager Ron Greenwood

" Dumbarton player Steve McCahill has
limped off with a badly cut forehead. "
Scottish radio journalist Tom Ferrie

" A contract on a piece of paper, saying you
want to leave, is like a piece of paper
saying you want to leave. "
Former Chelsea manager John Hollins

Football

" In terms of the Richter Scale this defeat
was a force eight gale. "
Former West Ham United manager John Lyall

" In comparison, there's no comparison. "
Ron Greenwood

I would also think that the action replay
showed it to be worse than it actually was.
Ron Atkinson

" Mirandinha will have more shots this
afternoon than both sides put together. "
Newcastle United legend Malcolm Macdonald

" Certain people are for me and certain
people are pro me. "
Terry Venables

Football

" What I said to them at half-time would be
unprintable on the radio. "
Former Tottenham manager Gerry Francis

" John Harkes going to Sheffield, Wednesday. "
New York Post

" If there weren't such a thing as football,
we'd all be frustrated footballers. "
Former Everton captain Mick Lyons

" The crowd think that Todd handled the ball. They
must have seen something that nobody else did. "
Barry Davies

They compare Steve McManaman to
Steve Heighway and he's nothing like
him, but I can see why – it's because
he's a bit different.
Kevin Keegan

" Glenn Hoddle hasn't been the Hoddle
we know. Neither has Bryan Robson. "
Ron Greenwood

There's no way Ryan Giggs is another
George Best. He's another Ryan Giggs.
Scottish legend Denis Law

" I don't think there is anybody bigger
or smaller than Maradona. "
Kevin Keegan

" What disappointed me was that we didn't play
with any passion. I'm not disappointed, you know,
I'm just disappointed. "
Kevin Keegan

" They had to get the brassieres to thaw it out. "
Ken Jones discussing a frozen pitch

Football

" Arsenal's width comes from wide areas. "
Jamie Redknapp is spaced out?

" 80 per cent of teams who score first in matches
go on to win them. But they may draw some
– or occasionally lose. "
David Pleat

" The referee looks at his whistle. "
Football commentator Dave Woods

" Well, Harry, fifth place last year,
how can you better that? "
Fergus Sweeney

Macclesfield have come out in the second
half with all guns steaming.
**Hot air in the commentary box
from Brian Seymour-Smith**

Football

Commentator 1: Looks like he's pulled his groin and has to come off.
Commentator 2: Yeah, he must have done it during the one or two touches he's had in this game...
Two BBC commentators debating how Liverpool's Maxi Rodriguez got his injury

Today was about our lack of ability to not produce the ability that we've got.
Hope West Ham manager Sam Allardyce's team talks are more clear cut

" I look forward to hearing from the silent majority."
Former manager-turned-pundit Alex McLeish is listening carefully

Football

" In the papers this morning: 'police closing in on Ian Holloway'. Sorry, 'Palace closing in on Ian Holloway'. "
Football pundit Alan Brazil

" I haven't seen it, but it looks generous. "
Arsenal manager Arsene Wenger seems psychic

The title race is between two horses and a little horse that needs milk and needs to learn how to jump. Maybe next season we can race.
Chelsea manager Jose Mourinho on Chelsea's title credentials

" He's been like a fresh of breath air. "
Manchester United legend-turned-pundit Roy Keane

" Berbatov put the penalty away like he was putting a penalty away. "
Chris Kamara is definite about the penalty

" Paolo Di Canio is one picnic short of a hamper. "
Alan Brazil

Whoever you support, you've got that blood
in your veins.
Former player Phil Neal's bloody right

" In the end, Rosicky initially did well. "
Andy Townsend gets a little mixed up

" Paolo di Canio managed with a bar of iron. "
Former Arsenal midfielder Paul Merson

" I think Southampton will finish above teams
that are well below them. "
Paul Merson again

" He could see the whites of the goals. "
**Former Liverpool player Jamie Redknapp
gets his metaphors in a twist**

" Arsenal needed to get a result at White Hart Lane like they did last year, albeit they were at home. "
Sky Sport's Redknapp strikes again

" This is a once-in-a-lifetime opportunity, but at least we've got another game on Tuesday. "
Marvin Sordell's inopportune comment

There is no precedent for what Suarez did, other than he's done it before.
An unprecedented comment from pundit and ex-player Danny Mills

" One or two Scotland players have got to look themselves in the face. "
Alan Brazil will get his fellow countrymen seeing double

" It's turning into a war of nutrition in midfield. "
**Food for thought from ex-Arsenal star
Martin Keown**

" Sandro's holding his face. You can tell
from that it's a knee injury. "
**You can tell Dion Dublin was a footballer
and not a doctor**

" Brendan Rodgers has been singing the praises
of Suarez and Sturridge – the SS. "
Perhaps Alan Brazil shouldn't mention the war

Sir Alex is going to be such a big, big,
big hole to replace.
Steve Bruce voids Ferguson's career

" Phil Dowd checks his whistle
and blows his watches. "
Commentator Alan Green

" Giroud scored with a brilliant header
with the last kick of the game."
Chris Kamara doesn't know his feet from his head

His brother-in-law is Scott Parker,
so he's got a good pedigree.
David Pleat mucks up a family tree

" After Chelsea scored, Bolton epitulated."
Paul Merson has a verbal capitulation on air

" Javier Chevanton don't speak the language
too good."
Neither does ex-player and manager Kevin Bond

" Does Di Canio look like Jimmy Nesbitt, or is it
Jimmy Nesbitt who looks like Di Canio?"
Mick Quinn's identity crisis

Football

" I can never predict my future because a
big part of my future is already behind me. "
**Back to the future for ex-Chelsea boss
Guus Hiddink**

" There's been a lot of pavola about that whole
Beckham thing... "
Brian Kerr makes a right palaver of this comment

" Scoring goals is the hardest thing in football but
doing it in a struggling team is even harder. "
Paul Merson states the obvious

Usmanov has got loads of money – we know
that from his wealth.
**Darren Gough is counting the cost
of this piece of silliness**

If that happens anywhere else on the pitch, it's a stonewall penalty.
Does Chris Kamara need a refresher course on the rules of the game?

" It was a no-needful tackle from Danny Fox. "
Manchester United's Phil Neville needs a dictionary

" If QPR go into the Championship, the players will be like rats jumping over a ship. "
Mick Quinn watches out for high-flying rodents at Loftus Road

" Wes Brown stepped into the plate today. "
Niall Quinn sees some crockery on the pitch

" You need to take off your rose-scented glasses. "
Smells like a comment from BBC pundit Robbie Savage

" There are fractions within the Manchester City dressing room. "
Danny Mills tells only part of the story

" Only one thing can stop Luis Suarez from being voted as the Players' Player of the Year – his fellow players. "
Jamie Redknapp states the obvious

" You have to put your shoes in Daniel Levy's shoes. "
Mick Quinn is in a tight spot

" Ricky Lambert's brain is very clever. "
Paul Merson

For me, Loic Remy is the key to this goal.
Strangely, Jamie Redknapp had it right because Remy had scored

" Berahino hasn't been the best player on
the pitch but he's my Man of the Match. "
**Owen Hargreaves doesn't quite understand the
concept of Man of the Match**

" Sometimes you've got to swallow the bullet. "
**Ex-player Brian Little shoots himself in the foot
with a metaphor**

It was handbags at half-mast.
**Newcastle manager Alan Pardew had better not
tell the Royal Navy**

" Tony Fernandes is in that goldfish bowl
and he's swimming against the tide. "
Former player Niall Quinn is talking wet

" That's a yellow card for Cazorla. So the next time
he's involved in Europe, he won't be. "
George Hamilton loses his normal verbal agility

Football

" Wilshere looks like he's got the grit between his teeth. "
BBC's Darren Gough leaves a nasty taste in the Arsenal midfielder's mouth

" Swansea are in cloud dreamland. "
Clarke Carlisle has his head in the clouds

" It was six of a half and one dozen of the other. "
Danny Higginbotham

" It's all pumps blazing as we go to the wire. "
Too many metaphors can be David Pleat's downfall

There's no such thing as a must-win game, and this is one of them.
Former player Alan Wright gets tongue-tied

Football

" We couldn't defend a fish supper. "
Sam Allardyce chips in with a
comment about his team

" Gareth Bale has been levitated to the status
of one of the best players in the world. "
Perry Groves reckons Bale is a high flier

" Any side in the world would miss Bareth Gale. "
David Pleat finds Gareth Bale a tongue twister

I think the next United manager is already
at the club. It could be either Ryan Giggs or
Ole Gunnar Solksjaer, who isn't at the club.
Michael Gray

" It's great to get that duck off my back. "
Chelsea and England's Gary Cahill

> Sidwell, Parker and Duff are all coming back
> to pastures old, as the saying goes.
> **Stan Collymore puts an old slant on an old adage**

" Big Sam has played his last dice."
Chris Kamara is a real card when it comes to gaffes

" N'Zonzi... so cool there, he didn't batter
an eyelid."
Commentator Gareth Owen

" If he scores, it's a different kettle of story."
Adrian Chiles was trying to speak metaphorically

" Villa were playing against defenders with
no confidence, then they took whatever
confidence they had left."
Kevin Keegan was quite confident about that

" Muller is non-stop perpetual motion. "
**Former player Graeme Souness is non-stop
on superlatives**

" I got a text from my daughter saying
she was having contraptions. "
**Peterborough boss Barry Fry gets tongue-
tied over becoming a grandad**

Who'll win the league? It's a coin toss between
three of them.
Ex-Southampton star Matt Le Tissier

" Karl Henry's got himself sent off for
a deliberate red card. "
Chris Kamara needs sending off for this one

" Are Spurs title contenders for the league? "
Mick Quinn poses a difficult question

" The possession stats at one point were
77 per cent to 33 per cent."
**Mick Quinn always gives 110 per cent in his
summarizing**

" In the last year, 46 of the 92 managers have lost
their jobs – that's over half."
Nearly, David Pleat, nearly

" A game is not won until it is lost."
You can't argue with David Pleat on that one

" I saw a defeat coming when they went 3-0 down."
David Pleat didn't need a crystal ball

His ability was natural and that's what you call
natural ability.
Kevin Keegan is right, naturally

Football

" Tottenham have lost all their European
quarter finals since they last won one. "
Commentator Clive Tyldesley

" The Villa keeper, Brad Goujon... "
Mick Quinn reckons Brad Guzan is tasty

Manchester City are going to go and win the
Premier League this year, as long as they can
get their complacency right.
Paul Merson

" West Brom haven't got the money to leave
people roasting in the reserves. "
**Competition for places is hot at the
Baggies according to Paul Merson**

" I come first, not football. "
Cristiano Ronaldo

Football

" I came in 11 years ago. I remember
it like it was tomorrow. "
**Time stood still for David Moyes when
he was Everton's manager**

" Sometimes he does the brilliant things really well. "
Ex-Manchester United player Lee Sharpe

" Tony Adams is braised for rejection by Arsenal. "
Alan Brazil sees the centre back done to a turn

" Sir Alex Ferguson is tough shoes to follow. "
Mick Quinn puts his foot in it

" You often see shocks in the League Cup, even
when you don't expect them. "
Commentator and ex-Liverpool player Jan Molby

" I'm a totally normal guy. I'm the Normal One. "
Jurgen Klopp

" When they don't score, they hardly ever win. "
**Michael Owen's searing insight on
Manchester City**

" The fans, they're tired of eating shit and shutting
their mouths. They will enjoy this, I promise. "
**Massimo Cellino on taking over as Leeds
chairman in 2014**

Tonight, we feel rubbish. OK, we feel shit.
**Jurgen Klopp after Liverpool lost the Capital One
Cup Final**

" They are the best invention ever. "
**Barry Hearn, Leyton Orient chairman after losing
a Play-Offs Final in 2001**

" If we close Sunderland – if we put a China Wall
around the city – it would be fantastic. "
Gus Poyet

" Yes, why wouldn't he be? He didn't have the baby. Unless he's breastfeeding he should be alright. "
Roy Keane, Republic of Ireland assistant manager, on Robbie Keane's availability after becoming a dad

" I think boring is ten years without a title – that's very boring. "
Jose Mourinho takes a sly dig at Arsene Wenger

" I was unhappy with my medical staff. They were impulsive and naïve. "
Jose Mourinho

I've never been in tears before but this was for a special reason.
Dick Advocaat after Sunderland survived relegation

Football

" Nandos isn't a nandos without fanta and coke mixed #fantoke."
Dele Alli

" All this tippy tappy stuff everybody keeps going on about as the right way to play is all a load of b******s."
Sam Allardyce

" I am a mountain goat that keeps going and going and going, I cannot be stopped, I just keep going."
Sepp Blatter before he was ousted as FIFA president

That is someone who should be given the Nobel Peace Prize. His contribution to the global humanitarian sphere is colossal.
Valdimir Putin on Blatter

I feel like my work was betrayed.
Jose Mourinho on his final match as Chelsea manager

" I've never been so certain about anything in my life. I want to be a coach. Or a manager. Not sure about which."
Phil Neville

" The run of the ball is not in our court at the moment."
Phil Neal

" Believe it or not, goals can change a game."
Mick Channon

" Peter Shilton conceded five, you don't get many of those to the dozen."
Des Lynam

Football

" We've got nothing to lose, and there's no point losing this game. "
Bobby Robson

" When the seagulls follow the trawler, it is because they think sardines will be thrown into the sea. "
Eric Cantona at his most enigmatic

" He's six foot something, fit as a flea, good looking – he's got to have something wrong with him. Hopefully he's hung like a hamster. "
Ian Holloway on Cristiano Ronaldo

" That's great. Tell him he's Pele and get him back on "
Partick Thistle manager John Lambie upon hearing his concussed striker didn't know who he was

Football

" Leicester have scored the first goal, which means they are 1-0 up. If it stays like this, they win."
Michael Owen is the master of the obvious

" Bolton have won just three of their last two games."
Commentator Ian Abrahams

Athletics

For some unknown reason
athletics attracts its fair share of
commentary calamities and bitchy
backbiting, so whether it be track or
field there is always somebody
putting their foot in it.

> In a moment we hope to see the pole vault over the satellite.
> **David Coleman has high expectations**

" She's dragged the javelin back into the twentieth century."
Ron Pickering

" One of the great unknown champions because very little is known about him."
David Coleman

" He's got to stick the boot in, to use a technical term."
Athlete Steve Ovett

" I am still looking for shoes that will make running on streets seem like running barefoot across the bosoms of maidens."
Dave Bronson, US marathon runner

Athletics

" What will my country give me if I win
100 metres gold in Sydney? Tobago probably. "
Ato Boldon, Trinidad and Tobago sprinter

" I don't think the discus will generate any
interest until they let us start throwing
them at one another. "
Al Oerter

" The late start is due to the time. "
David Coleman

" That's the fastest time ever run
– but it's not as fast as the world record. "
David Coleman

Behind every good decathlete,
there's a good doctor.
Bill Toomey

" Seb Coe is a Yorkshireman. So he's a complete
bastard and will do well in politics. "
Daley Thompson

" Italian men and Russian women
do not shave before a race. "
Eddie Ottoz, Italian athlete

" The decathlon is nine Mickey Mouse events and
the 1500 metres. "
Steve Ovett

When I lost my decathlon world record
I took it like a man. I only cried for ten hours.
Daley Thompson

" She's not Ben Johnson, but then who is? "
David Coleman

A very powerful set of lungs, very much hidden by that chest of his.
Athlete Alan Pascoe

" Running for money doesn't make you run fast. It makes you run first. "
Ben Jipcho, Kenyan athlete

" The best moment since I caught my tit in a mangle. "
Daley Thompson on winning Olympic gold in 1984

" Henry Rono, the man with those tremendous asbestos lungs. "
Ron Pickering

" He's a well balanced athlete; he has a chip on both shoulders. "
Derek Redmond on Linford Christie

" Being a decathlete is like having ten girlfriends. You have to love them all, and you can't afford losing one. "
Daley Thompson

He is going up and down like a metronome.
Ron Pickering

" There is Brendan Foster, by himself with 20,000 people. "
David Coleman

" And the hush of anticipation is rising to a crescendo. "
Ron Pickering

" I'm absolutely thrilled and over the world about it. "
Athlete Tessa Sanderson

" ...and finally she tastes the sweet smell of success. "
Ian Edwards

" I know I'm no Kim Basinger, but she can't throw a javelin. "
Fatima Whitbread

Watch the time. It gives you an indication of how fast they are running.
Ron Pickering

" The British team need to pull their socks out. "
Steve Cram

" Any press is good press. So keep on ragging me. "
Carl Lewis throws down a challenge

Athletics

" I started running in high school. I found out if you can run fast then you can get girls. "
Kim Collins

" I became a great runner because if you're a kid in Leeds and your name is Sebastian you've got to become a great runner. "
Lord Coe

World records are only borrowed.
Lord Coe

" When you go into an indoors championship like this, it's different to the outdoors. "
cs coach Max Jones

" It's a great advantage to be able to hurdle with both legs. "
David Coleman

" Running is a lot like life. Only 10% is exciting.
90% of it is slog and drudge. "
David Bedford

" First is first, and second is nowhere. "
Ian Stewart

You have to forget your last marathon before you
try another. Your mind can't know what's coming.
Frank Shorter, US marathon runner

" Ingrid Kristiansen, then, has smashed the world
record, running the 5,000 metres in 14:58.89.
Truly amazing. Incidentally, this is a personal best
for Ingrid Kristiansen. "
David Coleman

" Life is about timing. "
Carl Lewis

Athletics

" False start from Darsha – it was almost
as though she went before the gun went. "
cs commentator Paul Dickinson
seems unsure of the principle of false starts

" She's letting her legs do the running. "
**A detached view from athlete-turned-
commentator Brendan Foster**

It's a lovely sunny day here in the studio.
Channel 4 athletics presenter Ortis Deley

" He's 31 this year. Last year he was 30. "
BBC commentator David Coleman

" The Italians are hoping for an Italian victory. "
David Coleman

" The gold, silver and bronze will be won by
one of these five. "
David Coleman stumbles over his numbers

Well, Phil, tell us about your amazing third leg.
We think television presenter Ross King was discussing relays with champion runner Phil Redmond

" And there goes Juantorena down the back straight, opening his legs and showing his class. "
Athletics commentator Ron Pickering

" He just can't believe what's not happening to him. "
David Coleman clearly isn't seeing what is happening either

" It's your peripheral vision that goes when you're really exhausted; it's impossible to see anything directly in front of you. "
Blind panic for athlete and commentator Sally Gunnell

…and today is the night.
**It's all as plain as day (or was it night?)
for David Coleman**

" Zola Budd – so small, so waif-like,
you literally can't see her. But there she is. "
Commentator Alan Parry

" The theme of this year's race is Robin Hood,
so here to start us off are the Three Musketeers. "
**The race announcer at the Nottingham
Marathon gets lost in literary history**

" She went off so fast she literally died
in the last 50m. "
**Let's hope Sally Gunnell called
an ambulance, then**

" She's literally flying on a cloud! "
**Jessica Ennis's pole vault form was reaching
stratospheric heights for radio commentator
Katherine Merry**

" Linford Christie's got a habit of pulling
it out when it matters most. "
David Coleman

Rose's brain will now be telling him
exactly what to do.
A no-brainer for Ron Pickering

" Marion Jones was not flying with all her
engines blazing. "
Metaphors from athletics legend Steve Cram

Athletics

" And I can confirm that that's the fastest time
in the world this year for Radcliffe – and she
had to do it herself."
David Coleman sees Paula is getting no help

" Marion Jones was head and feet above everyone."
**Athlete and commentator John Regis obviously
looks up to the champion runner**

" That was an impressive run by the two English
runners – one running for England and the
other for Wales."
**David Coleman might just have offended
someone's national pride**

Nobody has ever won the title twice before. He
[Roger Black] has already done that.
**Has he or hasn't he? David Coleman
confuses us all**

> I think there is no doubt, she'll probably qualify for the final.
> **Surely David Coleman is sure?**

" The girls are all very tired. They have had six big events between their legs already."
Sally Gunnell

" Britain's last gold medal was a bronze in 1952 in Helsinki."
All that glitters is not gold for commentator Nigel Starmer-Smith

" The reason Pinto is so far ahead is because he is going so quickly."
A Homer Simpson "Doh!" moment from athletics summarizer Charlie Spedding

" Steve Ovett, Sebastian Coe, Steve Cram – the vanguard of our cream..."
Ron Pickering

" The Americans sowed the seed and
now they have reaped the whirlwind. "
Sebastian Coe

The Republic of China – back in the
Olympic Games for the first time.
David Coleman

" This evening is a very different evening from
the morning that we had this morning. "
**Sometimes David Coleman is not sure
of the time of day**

" Once he'd gone past the point of no return,
there was no going back. "
**There was no going back for a tongue-tied
BBC athletics commentator**

Athletics

" He is accelerating all the time. That last lap
was run in 64 seconds and the one before in 62. "
**David Coleman seems to be having trouble
with his stopwatch**

" Cram nailed his colours to the mast
and threw down the Great Pretender. "
Ron Pickering

" Mixed fortunes favour the brave. "
David Coleman

This is a young man who is only 25, and
you have to say, he has answered every
question that has ever been asked.
David Coleman

Mary Decker Slaney, the world's greatest front runner – I shouldn't be surprised to see her at the front.
Ron Pickering

" Christie clearly has hamstring trouble, we think."
David Coleman is hamstrung for clarity

" This is a truly international field, no Britons involved."
David Coleman

" The Americans' heads are on their chins a little bit at the moment."
Things are a bit topsy-turvy for Ron Pickering

" I have the feeling that Machado is an athlete who likes to get away from the opposition."
David Coleman reckons that athlete Machado Manuela is a runaway success

Athletics

" She hasn't run faster than herself before."
Athlete and commentator Zola Budd

" Born in America, John returned to his native Japan."
**Long distance runner Mike Gratton needs
some geography lessons**

" We estimate, and this isn't an estimation,
that Greta Waitz is 80 seconds behind."
David Coleman

" And there's no 'I love you' message because
Steve Ovett has married the girl."
Does David Coleman not understand romance?

The Kenyans haven't done much in the last
two games, in fact they haven't competed
since 1972.
Brendan Foster

" And there you see Sebastian Coe
preparing for our first look at him. "
Jim Rosenthal

" Some names to look forward to
– perhaps in the future. "
David Coleman

It's a battle with himself and with
the ticking finger of the clock.
David Coleman

" And with alphabetical irony Nigeria
follows New Zealand. "
David Coleman

" There you can see her parents. Her
father died a long time ago. "
Does David Coleman see ghosts?

Athletics

" He's running on his nerve ends. "
BBC commentator Peter West.
Ouch, that must hurt!

" Coe has smashed the world record
– 1:44.92 has never been run easier. "
Ron Pickering

" I ran like a lemon and lemons don't run. "
A sour note for British 400m runner
Daniel Caines after a poor performance

" Moses Kiptanui, the 19-year-old Kenyan
who turned 20 a few weeks ago. "
David Coleman

And the crowd is absolutely standing in their seats.
Ron Pickering

And the line-up for the final of the women's 400m hurdles includes three Russians, two East Germans, a Pole, a Swede and a Frenchman.
Well observed by David Coleman

" He is even smaller in real life than he is on the track. "
David Coleman

" And the mile once again becomes the focal point where it's always been. "
Ron Pickering

" We keep thinking we have reached the bottom but then we find a new bottom. But I think we have reached the last bottom possible. "
American sprinter Michael Johnson on the Great Britain athletics team's bum performances

" He only needs to be last in this. "
BBC commentator David Vine
covering athletics

Ian Mackie is here to prove his back
injury is behind him.
Anonymous radio commentator

" He's got so much potential and most of
it still to be realised? "
Commentator Stuart Storey is waiting
for a good performance

" [Steve] Backley must be looking forward to
the world championships, the title really could
go to anyone that's there. "
David Coleman hedging his bets

" Is there something that sticks out that makes you an exceptional pole vaulter?"
Television presenter Adrian Chiles deserves some stick for this comment

" Basically, we are not human, we dropped from space like Mr Bean. Mr Bean is not a normal guy; he makes jokes. We are not normal guys. We are from space, I am from Mars."
Sprinter Yohan Blake thinks his Jamaican team was out of this world at the 2012 Olympic Games

Is that a grimace of pain in his right knee?
Commentator-turned-"medical expert" David Coleman

" The whole case smells of a political hit job and nothing more."
Artyom Patsev after WADA's investigation into doping in Russia

I just imagine all the other runners are big spiders, and then I get super scared.
Usain Bolt

" I spent 12 years training for a career that was over in one week. Joe Namath spent one week training for a career that lasted 12 years."
Bruce Jenner, US decathlete

" My son Linford does not take drugs. If they said he was taking roast chicken and baked potatoes then I would believe that."
James Christie, Linford Christie's father

" I wouldn't be surprised if one day Carl Lewis's halo slipped and choked him."
Allan Wells

> It's only jumping into a sandpit.
> **Jonathan Edwards on his world-record triple jump**

" You don't run 26 miles at five minutes a mile on good looks and a secret recipe. "
Frank Shorter, US marathon runner

" You have to be suspicious when you line up against girls with moustaches. "
Maree Holland, Australian 400m runner

" An athlete cannot run with money in his pockets. He must run with hope in his heart and dreams in his head. "
Emil Zatopek

Athletics

" Why couldn't Pheidippides have died here?"
**Frank Shorter's comment to a teammate at the
16-mile mark in one of his first marathons**

" You won't win silver medals at the Olympic Games
unless you're the very best."
Pat Glenn

Boxing

Boxers can deliver as many knock-out blows with their tongues as with their fists. With the action outside the ring being as intense as that inside, it's seconds out.

George Foreman is so ugly he should donate his face to the US Bureau of Wildlife.
Muhammad Ali

" It's just a job. Grass grows, birds fly, waves pound the sand. I beat people up. "
Muhammad Ali

" I'm so fast that last night I turned off the light switch in my hotel room and was in bed before the room was dark. "
Muhammad Ali

" I'm going to fade into Bolivian. "
Former heayweight champion Mike Tyson

" You can sum up this sport in two words: 'You never know. "
Veteran boxing trainer Lou Duva

" I've seen George Foreman shadow boxing
and the shadow won."
Muhammad Ali

" There's a cliché in boxing – records are only for DJs."
Dereck Chisora's coach Don Charles on records

Well, a tiger does not lose sleep over the
opinion of a sheep.
**Carl Froch doesn't worry about
rival Adonis Stevenson**

" I sometimes feel like I'm the Miley Cyrus
of heavyweight boxing – young, crazy, super
sexy & don't give a ****."
Tyson Fury

" I truly believe that the confidence I have is
unbelievable."
Prince Naseem Hamed

Boxing

" Sure, there have been injuries and deaths in boxing
– but none of them serious. "
Former champion Alan Minter

" He's a guy who gets up at 6 a.m. regardless
of what time it is. "
Veteran boxing trainer Lou Duva

My mum says I used to fight my way out of
the cot. But I can't remember. That was before
my time.
Former heavyweight champion Frank Bruno

" I'm only a prawn in the game. "
British boxer Brian London

" The British Press hate a winner who's British.
They don't like any British man to have balls
as big as a cow's, like I have. "
Nigel Benn

" Do I believe in superstitions? No. If you have superstitions, that's bad luck. "
Canadian middleweight Eric Lucas

I quit school in the sixth grade because of pneumonia. Not because I had it, but because I couldn't spell it.
Rocky Graziano

" Not being born to parents who were accountants was probably my biggest mistake. "
Chris Eubank

" For ageing boxers, first your legs go. Then your reflexes go. Third, your friends go. "
Willie Pep

Boxing is like jazz. The better it is,
the less people appreciate it.
George Foreman

" No, I don't mind the fight being at three in the
morning. Everyone in Glasgow fights at three in
the morning. "
Jim Watt

" All fighters are prostitutes and all promoters
are pimps. "
Larry Holmes

" It's not bragging if you can back it up. "
Muhammad Ali

" He's standing there making a sitting target
of himself. "
Terry Lawless

Boxing

" The chances of a rematch for Lewis are slim
and none. And slim is out of town. "
Don King

To me, boxing is like ballet except there's
no music, no choreography and the
dancers hit each other.
Jack Handey

" We'll have to take it on the chin. It's a
real body blow. "
British promoter Barry Hearn

" So over to the ringside – Harry Commentator is
your carpenter. "
BBC announcer

" If you even dream of beating me you'd better
wake up and apologise. "
Muhammad Ali

Boxing

" There's more to boxing than hitting. There's
not getting hit, for instance. "
George Foreman hits the nail on the head

" Chris Eubank is as genuine as a three-dollar bill. "
Mickey Duff

I want to rip out his heart and feed it to him.
I want to kill people. I want to rip their stomachs
out and eat their children.
Mike Tyson

" The three toughest fighters I've ever been
up against were Sugar Ray Robinson, Sugar
Ray Robinson, and Sugar Ray Robinson.
I fought Sugar so many times, I'm surprized
I'm not diabetic! "
Jake LaMotta

Boxing

" I don't think you can compare like with like. "
Boxing promoter Frank Warren reckons it's beyond comparison

" To be honest it was a very physical fight. "
Jim Watt

" Lennox Lewis fought the perfect fight.
He just got hit on the chin. "
Lennox Lewis's trainer following his fighter's shock world title defeat

There's going to be a real ding-dong
when the bell goes.
David Coleman

" I can only see it going one way, that's my way.
How it's actually going to go I can't really say. "
British amateur boxer Nick Wilshire

Boxing

" His face was a mask of blood. I think he must have a cut somewhere. "
British boxing legend Henry Cooper

" Frank Bruno's strength, in fact, is his strength. "
Boxing commentator Reg Gutteridge

" Born in Italy, most of his fights have been in his native New York. "
TV presenter Des Lynam

" I would like to retire with brains still in contact. "
Boxer Herol Graham

" I'm concentrating so much I don't know what I'm doing myself half the time. "
Former British middleweight Mark Kaylor

I stand a 50-50 chance if not 50-60 against anyone out there.
Frank Bruno needs a maths refresher course

Boxing

" I've had 38 fights, lost one and was never
put on my feet. "
Boxing's topsy-turvy for Gary Mason

" Marvellous oriental pace he's got,
just like a Buddhist statue. "
Harry Carpenter

" I think it was the clash of styles that made
it a good fight; we both have similar styles. "
**Perhaps a clash of heads meant Lennox
Lewis wasn't thinking straight**

Mike Tyson will have to go into a room by himself
and get used to seeing the outside world again.
Frank Bruno's thinking is inside out maybe?

" He looks up at him through
blood-smeared lips. "
Boxing commentator Harry Carpenter

" I never cease to amaze myself. I say this humbly. "
Self-effacing as ever, US boxing promoter
Don King

" I've only ever seen Errol Christie fight once before
and that was the best I've ever seen him fight. "
Mark Kaylor

I'll fight Lloyd Honeyghan for nothing,
if the price is right.
Marlon Starling

" I'm not the Greatest; I'm the Double Greatest.
Not only do I knock them out, I pick the round. "
Muhammad Ali

Boxing

I had Bernard Taylor five rounds ahead going into their fifth round.
Former boxer-turned-commentator Alan Minter

" Pedroza, the crown on his head hanging by a thread..."
Harry Carpenter

" No fighter comes into the ring hoping to win – he goes in hoping to win."
Henry Cooper

" They said it would last two rounds – they were half right, it lasted four."
Harry Carpenter

" It's not one of Bruno's fastest wins... but it's one of them."
Harry Carpenter isn't too sure

Boxing

> The Mexicans... these tiny little men
> from South America...
> **Harry Carpenter needs a geography lesson**

" Now it comes to a simple equation:
who can stand the heat?"
Harry Carpenter

" I don't know what impressive is,
but Joe was impressive tonight."
**It's not hard to impress boxer
Joe Bugner's wife Marlene –
once she's grasped what it means**

" Magri has to do well against the unknown
Mexican who comes from a famous family
of five boxing brothers."
Harry Carpenter

" Venezuela? Great! That's the Italian city
with the guys in the boats, right?"
**US boxing promoter Murad Muhammad
is a bit geographically challenged**

We have an all-American boy here,
even though he is a Canadian.
**National boundaries don't matter for promoter
Billy Joe Fox when talking about signing
heavyweight boxer Willie de Wit**

" I believe a woman's best place is in the kitchen and
on her back."
**Boxer Tyson Fury stunned the world when
winning the heavyweight championship and
then did so again with some of his more
outrageous comments**

You're boring and I want to get you out of the heavyweight division. You have about as much charisma as my underpants. Zero.
Tyson Fury on Wladimir Klitschko

" I should be a postage stamp. That's the only way I'll ever get licked. "
Muhammad Ali

" Don King doesn't care about black and white. He cares about green. "
Larry Holmes

" Inside of a ring or out, ain't nothing wrong with going down. It's staying down that's wrong. "
Muhammad Ali

" Frank Bruno says I'm chicken. Well, you can tell him I've come home to roost. "
Joe Bugner

Boxing

" Nigel Benn is like washing-up liquid: built on hype and one day the bubble will burst. "
Chris Eubank

" This boxer is doing what's expected of him, bleeding from the nose. "
Harry Carpenter

Wrestling and boxing is like Ping-Pong and rugby. There's no connection.
Actor Mickey Rourke

" I am the greatest. I said that even before I knew I was. I figured that if I said it enough, I would convince the world that I really was the greatest. "
Muhammad Ali

Golf

From the first tee to the nineteenth hole, golf is littered with some of the most bizarre comments. Strip away the veneer of polite etiquette and the gloves are certainly off. Fore!

" It's a funny old game. One day you're a statue,
the next you're a pigeon. "
Peter Alliss

" Nick Faldo is as much fun as Saddam Hussein. "
Scott Hoch

And now to hole eight, which is in fact
the eighth hole.
Peter Alliss

" I made the last putt. It just didn't go in. "
Golfer Tom Kite

" I could have chosen a better word. If I had gone
for lousy, that might have captured it better. "
**Faldo digging a hole over his comments
about Sergio Garcia**

That beautiful woman lives with me.
A rottweiler with lip-gloss.
Peter Alliss

" I disappeared down to the beach
after the Masters and lay on the
beach and cried."
**Greg Norman on accepting
defeat manfully**

" I owe a lot to my parents, especially my
mother and father."
Golf legend Greg Norman

" I think Steve is the nicest guy in
the world, too, so it couldn't happen
to a nicer guy."
Luke Donald on Steve Stricker

Golf

" Unfortunately the guys this afternoon will struggle with a few pin positions. Eighth hole is a joke, 18th needs a windmill and a clown face. "
Ian Poulter goes crazy

" We have had our behinds handed to us for seven of the last nine. That did not sit well with me. "
Tom Watson gets to the bottom of why he took on the Ryder Cup captaincy

" I try not to take anything now apart from Corona and vodka. "
Lee Westwood

It was my mum's birthday yesterday and I wanted to win it for her because I forgot to get her a present.
George Coetzee

He used to be fairly indecisive, but now he's not so certain.
Peter Alliss

" Difficult couple of holes here – 15, 16 and 17."
Former golfer Howard Clark

" I feel like punching myself."
Rory McIlroy

" If you are caught on a golf course during a storm and are afraid of lightning, hold up a 1-iron. Not even God can hit a 1-iron."
Lee Trevino

" Ballesteros felt much better today after a 69."
Golf commentator Renton Laidlaw

" 'What do I think of Tiger Woods?' I don't know.
I never played there. "
Golfer Sandy Lyle

" I'm not saying my golf game went bad, but
if I grew tomatoes they'd come up sliced. "
Lee Trevino

We've had it easy. When it blows here [St
Andrews] even the seagulls walk.
Nick Faldo

" When Seve gets his Porsche going, not even
San Pedro in heaven could stop him. "
**Jose Maria Olazabal on the
unstoppable Ballesteros**

" The only thing a golfer needs is more daylight. "
Ben Hogan

Golf

" We're going to have to start giving the Americans handicap strokes. This is getting boring. "
Sandy Lyle after another European Ryder Cup victory in 2006

" If you'd offered me a 69 at the start this morning I'd have been all over you. "
Golfer Sam Torrance

Azinger is wearing an all-black outfit: black jumper, blue trousers, white shoes and a pink tea-cosy hat.
Renton Laidlaw

" I can tell you now that I'll know exactly when I want to retire; but when I reach that time I may not know. "
Jack Nicklaus

Golf

I played so good, it was like the hole kept getting in the way of my ball.
Calvin Peete

" They call it golf because all the other four-letter words were taken. "
Raymond Floyd

" Like an octopus falling out of a tree. "
David Feherty on Jim Furyk's swing

" I don't like golf. It's not for me, it's too quiet. "
Mario Balotelli

" You can make a lot of money in this game. Just ask my ex-wives. Both of them are so rich that neither of their husbands work. "
Lee Trevino

Golf

" One of the reasons Arnie Palmer is playing
so well is that, before each final round, his
wife takes out his balls and kisses them.
Oh my God, what have I just said?"
US Open TV commentator

He [Ernie Els] has just got engaged, which
is perhaps why he produced a 69 today.
**Is BBC golf correspondent Tony
Adamson getting a bit personal?**

" As the cock crows, it's only about 200 yards."
Golf commentator Peter Alliss

" A very small crowd here today. I can count the
people on one hand. Can't be more than 30."
Perhaps Michael Abrahamson has big hands?

Golf

" That was a beautiful shot.
Inch perfect – but an inch wide. "
**A BBC golf commentator just wasn't
measuring up on the day**

" Some weeks Nick likes to use Fanny;
other weeks he prefers to do it by himself. "
**Ken Brown talking about golfer
Nick Faldo's caddy Fanny Sunesson –
from a sporting point of view, of course**

" Pinero has missed the putt. I wonder
what he's thinking in Spanish? "
**BBC commentator Renton Laidlaw
wonders what "Oh, bugger" is in Spanish**

There he stands with his legs akimbo.
**Surely golf pundit Peter Alliss is
pulling someone's leg?**

Golf

Sandy Lyle talking to Tony Adamson,
a lifetime ambition fulfilled.
BBC commentator Ian Robertson

Peter Alliss: What do you think
of the climax of this tournament?
Peter Thomson: I'm speechless.
Alliss: That says it all.
**The BBC golf commentary team,
men of few words**

" This is the 12th, the green is like
a plateau with the top shaved off."
Renton Laidlaw goes a little flat

" Notices are appearing at courses telling
golfers not to lick their balls on the green."
**One commentator at the 1989 British Masters
golf tournament has got the double
entendre licked**

I made the last putt. It just didn't go in.
**Golfer Tom Kite on the difference
between victory and defeat**

" Yes, Jean van de Velde is a clown,
another Frère Jacques Cousteau. "
Oh, brother, is Tony Adamson mixed up!

" Birdies wherever you look. They're coming
down like hailstones. "
Former professional golfer Ken Brown

" That's not a million miles away. "
Peter Alliss

" And on the eve of the Bob Hope Classic
an interview with the man himself
– Gerald Ford. "
**Mistaken identity by golf
presenter Jim Rosenthal**

" You couldn't find two more different personalities than these two men, Tom Watson and Brian Barnes. One the complete golf professional and the other the complete professional golfer."
Peter Alliss

" It's for all the gold in the world."
Peter Alliss reckons there's a fortune in golf

Was I intimated by Tiger Woods? A little bit. He's got an aroma about him.
Ben Curtis can sniff out a winner

" The par here at Sunningdale is 70 and anything under that will be a score in the 60s."
Commentator Steve Rider has his maths right

Golf

" I can't see, unless the weather changes,
the conditions changing dramatically. "
Peter Alliss

" He certainly didn't appear as cool as he looked. "
Renton Laidlaw

" She is probably thinking, 'If this goes in, I get a
new kitchen'. "
Peter Alliss on Zach Johnson's wife, Kim

" He's a grizzled veteran at 21 years old – just 21.
Jordan is so beyond his years. "
Jack Nicklaus on Jordan Spieth

I mean the man who designed this golf course
had to have one leg shorter than the other.
**Gary Player was not too keen on Chambers
Bay, venue of the US Open**

If you're going to talk negative about a place, you're almost throwing yourself out to begin with, because golf is a mental game.
Jordan Spieth

" It's *Star Wars* golf. This place was designed by Darth Vader."
Ben Crenshaw on the Sawgrass course

" Augusta National is like playing a Salvador Dali landscape. I expected a clock to fall out of the trees and hit me in the face."
David Feherty goes surreal

" Foursomes have left the first tee there and have never been seen again. They just find their shoelaces and bags."
Bob Hope on Pine Valley GC

I'm glad I brought this course, this monster, to its knees.
Ben Hogan on Oakland Hills

" Pebble Beach is Alcatraz with grass. "
Bob Hope

" I feel like I'm back visiting an old grandmother. She's crotchety and eccentric, but also elegant. Anyone who doesn't fall in love with her has no imagination. "
Tony Lema on the Old Course at St. Andrews

" The women who are there as wives of husbands, they get all the facilities. If somebody wants to join, you better get married to someone who's a member. "
Peter Alliss courts controversy with his views on Muirfield's decision not to alloww female members to join the club

Golf

" That ball is so far left Lassie couldn't find it even if it was wrapped in bacon. "
David Feherty after a wayward Phil Mickelson drive

" I am not saying the greens are fast, but it's like they have been bikini-waxed. "
Gary McCord wasn't impressed by Augusta's greens

" Fortunately he is 22 years old, so his right wrist should be the strongest muscle in his body. "
David Feherty on Rory McIlroy

" I hit the ball as hard as I can. If I can find it, I hit it again. "
John Daly

Cricket

From brutal sledging out in the middle to the wit and wisdom up in the commentary box, cricket has many sides. Combining the risqué with the odd blunder it is truly a rich "seam" of content.

> The only time an Australian walks is when his car runs out of petrol.
> **Barry Richards**

" I remember the 1992 World Cup final. It's my earliest memory. Inzamam-ul-Haq was skinny. Well, skinny-ish. "
Moeen Ali's fond memories of Inzamam-ul-Haq

" He played a cut so late as to be positively posthumous. "
John Arlott

" Gatting at fine leg – that's a contradiction in terms. "
Richie Benaud

Cricket

" How can you tell your wife you are just
popping out to play a match and then
not come back for five days?"
Rafa Benitez on the finer points of cricket

" I can't really say I'm batting badly. I'm not
batting long enough to be batting badly."
Greg Chappell

Bill Frindall needs a small ruler. How about the
Sultan of Brunei? I hear he's only four foot ten.
Brian Johnston

" There were congratulations and high sixes
all round."
Richie Benaud

Cricket

" I have prepared for the worst-case scenario, but it could be even worse than that."
England spin bowler Monty Panesar

" If this bloke's a Test Match bowler, then my backside is a fire engine."
David Lloyd on Kiwi, Nathan Astle, who took more than 50 Test Match wickets

" More brains in a pork pie."
Geoff Boycott on Kevin Pietersen

Ray Illingworth has just relieved himself at the Pavilion End.
Brian Johnston

" You can't get out any earlier than the second ball of the game."
David Lloyd

And we don't need a calculator to tell us that the run-rate required is 4.5454 per over.
Christopher Martin-Jenkins

" It is now possible they can get the impossible score they first thought possible."
CM-J on the art of the impossible

" He is a very dangerous bowler. Innocuous, if you like."
David Lloyd on Chris Harris

" It's never easy putting a rubber on, is it, Michael?"
Jonathan Agnew poses a tricky one for Michael Vaughan

Cricket

" It was as if he [Cook] still writes to Santa
Claus and puts his tooth under his pillow
for the tooth fairy. "
Pietersen on Alastair Cook

Get ready for a f****** broken arm.
**Michael Clarke welcoming Jimmy Anderson to
the crease**

" England finally cruised to a 2-0 series win over
Bangladesh through the batting of Alastair
Cook, who hit a 12th Test century, and
Kevin Pietersen. "
BBC Sport report

" Brian Toss won the close. "
BBC cricket commentator Henry Blofeld

" Admitting to being a Tory in Scotland is seen
as a bit weird like cross-dressing or liking cricket."
Fraser Nelson, *The Spectator* editor

" I always walked... bit hard to stand there with
all three stumps lying on the ground."
Glenn McGrath

" Punching lockers isn't the way forward for anyone.
There's only going to be one winner there."
Ben Stokes

There's only one head bigger than Tony Greig's
and that's Birkenhead.
Fred Trueman

" That slow-motion replay doesn't show how
fast the ball was travelling."
Richie Benaud

Cricket

" Yes, he's a very good cricketer – pity he's not a better batter or bowler. "
Former England cricketer Tom Graveney

" Cricket is baseball on valium. "
Robin Williams

I've done the elephant. I've done the poverty.
I might as well go home.
Phil Tufnell on Indian tour

" Chris Lewis is the enigma with no variation. "
Vic Marks

" To dismiss this lad Denness you don't have to bowl fast, you just have to run up fast. "
Brian Close

Cricket

Truly, I think I could get more runs if England had some faster bowlers.
Viv Richards

" And umpire Dickie Bird is gestating
wildly as usual."
Tony Lewis

" Pakistan is the sort of place every man should
send his mother-in-law to, for a month,
all expenses paid."
Ian Botham

" On the first day, Logie decided to chance his arm
and it came off."
Trevor Bailey

" You've got to make split-second decisions
so quickly."
Geoffrey Boycott

" I have never got to the bottom of streaking. "
Jonathan Agnew

I don't think I've actually drunk a beer for
15 years, except a few Guinnesses in Dublin,
where it's the law.
Ian Botham

" A few years ago England would have struggled
to beat the Eskimos. "
Ian Botham

" The other advantage England have got when
Phil Tufnell is bowling is that he isn't fielding. "
Ian Chappell

" The only person who could be better
than Brian Lara could be Brian Lara himself. "
Colin Croft

England have no McGrathish bowlers. There are hardly any McGrathish bowlers, except for [Glenn] McGrath.
Stuart Law

" I can't bat, can't bowl and can't field these days. I've every chance of being picked for England."
Essex spinner Ray East

" I'm ugly, I'm overweight, but I'm happy."
Andrew Flintoff

" I don't know an England player who could fix a light bulb, let alone a match."
Darren Gough

" Shane Warne's idea of a balanced diet is a cheeseburger in each hand."
Ian Healy

Cricket

" The blackcurrant jam tastes of fish to me. "
Derek Randall on caviar

The third umpires should be changed as often
as nappies… and for the same reason.
Navjot Sidhu

" I'd have looked even faster in colour. "
Fred Trueman

" As the ball gets softer it loses its hardness. "
Geoff Boycott

" I'm glad two sides of the cherry have
been put forward. "
Geoffrey Boycott

" I'm a big believer that the coach is something you
travel in to get to and from the game. "
Shane Warne, not a big fan of cricket coaching

Geoff Boycott has the uncanny knack of being where fast bowlers aren't.
Tony Greig

" They should cut Joel Garner off at the knees to make him bowl at a normal height. "
Geoff Boycott

" Unless something happens that we can't predict, I don't think a lot will happen. "
Fred Trueman

" It's a catch-21 situation. "
England batsman Kevin Pietersen

" Life without sports is like life without underpants. "
Cricket umpire Billy Bowden gets to the naked truth

Cricket

" I've been a bit of a useless tosser up to now."
Paul Collingwood's self-awareness

" Pakistan without Ajmal is like ice-cream
without chocolate topping."
Ian Chappell

" He's nearly 34 – in fact he's 33."
Richie Benaud

Pakistan can play well, but they have the ability to
play badly, too.
Cricket commentator John Emburey

" Sorry, skipper, a leopard can't change its stripes."
Former Australian cricketer Lennie Pascoe

" We've won one on the trot."
Former England cricket captain Alec Stewart

Like an elephant trying to do the pole vault.
Cricket commentator Jonathan Agnew on Inzaman-ul-Haq as the rotund Pakistan captain falls over his own stumps

" To stay in, you've got to not get out. "
Cricket commentator Geoffrey Boycott

" His tail is literally up! "
Cricket commentator Trevor Bailey

" Captaincy is 90% luck and 10% skill. But don't try it without that 10%. "
Cricket commentator Richie Benaud

" I sleep the whole day after breakfast to get in shape for the game. "
Chris Gayle

Cricket

I don't ask Kathy to face Michael
Holding. So I don't see why I should
be changing nappies.
Ian Botham on family duties

" It's only a matter of time before the end
of this innings. "
Michael Peschardt

" Unless somebody can pull a miracle out of the fire,
Somerset are cruising into the semi-final. "
Fred Trueman

" Don't bother looking for that, let alone chasing it.
That's gone straight into the confectionery stall
and out again. "
Cricket commentator Richie Benaud

Cricket

" And we have just heard, although this is not the latest score from Bournemouth, that Hampshire have beaten Nottinghamshire by nine wickets. "
Peter West

" The umpire signals a bye with the air of a weary stalk. "
Cricket commentator John Arlott

" Like an old lady poking with her umbrella at a wasp's nest. "
John Arlott on the batting style of Australian Ernie Toshack

It's especially tense for Parker, who's literally fighting for a place on an overcrowded plane to India.
Cricket commentator Trevor Bailey

Cricket

" This is Cunis at the Vauxhall End. Cunis –
a funny sort of name. Neither one thing
nor the other."
Alan Gibson

" Boycott, somewhat a creature of habit, likes
exactly the sort of food he himself prefers."
Dan Mosey

" The Port Elizabeth ground is more of a
circle than an oval. It is long and square."
Trevor Bailey

" Tavare has literally dropped anchor."
Trevor Bailey

A gun is no more dangerous than a
cricket bat in the hands of a madman.
Prince Philip

Cricket

" He's not quite got hold of that one. If he had,
it would have gone for nine. "
**Cricket commentator Richie Benaud
on a Justin Langer six**

" The first time you face up to a googly
you're going to be in trouble if you've
never faced one before. "
Trevor Bailey

" Clearly the West Indies are going to
play their normal game, which is what
they normally do. "
Tony Greig

Welcome to Worcester where you've just missed
seeing Barry Richards hitting one of Basil
D'Oliveira's balls clean out of the ground.
Brian Johnston

Cricket

" And Glenn McGrath dismissed for two, just
98 runs short of his century."
Richie Benaud

" There was a slight interruption
there for athletics."
Richie Benaud on a streaker

" Well, Wally, I've been watching this
game both visually and on TV."
Ken Barrington

" Andre Nel is big and raw-boned and I suspect he
has the IQ of an empty swimming pool."
Adam Parore

When there's a hosepipe ban covering three-
quarters of the country, you don't expect a
damp wicket at Lord's.
Bob Willis

Cricket

" This shirt is unique, there are only 200
of them. "
Richie Benaud

" Gavin Larsen is inexperienced in Test
cricket in that this is his first Test. "
Geoff Boycott

Denis Compton was the only player to
call his partner for a run and wish him
good luck at the same time.
England cricketer John Warr

" Our Cheese was out there, growing runny
in the heat. A Dairylea triangle thinking
he was Brie. "
Kevin Pietersen on Matt Prior

Cricket

" We welcome World Service listeners
to the Oval, where the bowler's Holding,
the batsman's Willey."
**BBC cricket commentator Brian Johnston
couldn't get to grips with this**

" And the rest not only is history but will
remain history for many years to come."
Commentator Jack Bannister

" And a sedentary seagull flies by."
It was obviously a slow day for Brian Johnston

" The lights are shining quite darkly."
**Maybe Henry Blofeld still had
his sunglasses on?**

" The crowd realizes there's a match on here."
**Commentator Ravi Shastri realizes
why so many people turned up for
an India v. Pakistan cricket game**

Cricket

" There were no scores below single figures. "
Former Australian cricket captain and
broadcaster Richie Benaud gets negative

As he comes in to bowl, Freddie Titmus
has got two short legs, one of them square.
Brian Johnston

" And Ian Greig's on eight, including two fours. "
England cricket legend Jim Laker

" Yorkshire 332 all out, Hutton ill – I'm sorry,
Hutton 111. "
Digits caused a problem for BBC newsreader
John Snagge

" The Queen's Park Oval – as its name suggests,
absolutely round! "
Geometry was not a strong point for
West Indian cricketer Tony Cozier

Cricket

" That was intentional from Gambhir."
Cricket commentator Ravi Shastri
as Gautam Gambhir hits a four

" His throw went absolutely nowhere
near where it was going."
Is this Richie Benaud's idea
of a near-miss?

" England have nothing to lose here,
apart from this Test match."
Former England cricketer and coach-
turned-commentator David Lloyd

We have had exceptionally wet weather
in Derby – everywhere in the county
is in the same boat.
Kenyan cricket chief Tom Sears

Cricket

" Pietersen is on the charge and on the pull. "
**Is David Lloyd putting adoring ladies
on alert for the England cricketer?**

" We didn't have metaphors in our day.
We didn't beat around the bush. "
Fred Trueman

The ball came back, literally cutting him in half.
Cricket commentator Colin Croft

" That black cloud is coming from the direction
the wind is blowing. Now the wind is coming
from where the black cloud is. "
**Perhaps it's best that former England
captain Ray Illingworth is now a cricket
commentator and not a weatherman**

Cricket

" In Hampshire's innings the Smith
brothers scored 13 and 52 respectively. "
Henry Blofeld

" The wicket didn't do too much, but when
it did, it did too much. "
Former England captain Mike Gatting

" Michael Vaughan has a long history in
the game ahead of him. "
Cricket broadcaster Mark Nicholas

" Gul has another ball in his hand and bowls
to Bell, who has two. "
Christopher Martin-Jenkins

This really is a fairy-book start.
Cricketer Bob Willis

And there's the George Headley stand,
named after George Headley.
South African cricket commentator Trevor Quirk

" England have a very English attack. "
Cricket commentator Geoffrey Boycott

" Gary never had a nickname – he was
always called either Gary or The King. "
Cricketer Pat Pocock

" He's usually a good puller, but that time
he couldn't get it up. "
**According to Richie Benaud,
someone needs Viagra**

" Laird has been brought in to stand
in the corner of the circle. "
**Richie Benaud needs to square
that circle somehow**

Cricket

Michael Atherton must think all his Christmases are coming home at once.
Maybe Geoff Boycott thought Santa Claus was next in to bat?

" Sean Pollock there, a carbon copy of his dad. Except he's a bit taller and he's got red hair. "
Cricket commentator Trevor Bailey

" There's Neil Harvey standing at leg slip with his legs wide apart, waiting for a tickle. "
This sort of thing is just not cricket for Brian Johnston

" I don't think he expected it, and that's what caught him unawares. "
Trevor Bailey

" I think if you've got a safe pair of hands, you've got a safe pair of hands. "
Cricket commentator Tom Graveney

Cricket

" Anyone foolish enough to predict the
outcome of this match is a fool. "
Fred Trueman

England might now be the favourites
to draw this match.
Spin bowler Vic Marks seems in a spin himself

" Mike Atherton's a thinking captain:
he gives the impression of someone
with his head on all the time. "
**Thinking is more than cricket commentator
Colin Croft was doing at the time**

" Fortunately it was a slow ball, so it wasn't
a fast one. "
Same as Geoff Boycott on this occasion?

Cricket

" Now Ramprakash is facing a fish of a rather different feather in Mark Waugh. "
Perhaps they were flying fish for cricket commentator Peter Baxter

Glen McGrath bowled so badly in his first test as though he'd never bowled in a Test match before.
Geoff Boycott puts our brains to the test

" Now Botham, with a chance to put everything that's gone before behind him. "
Tony Cozier

" Courtney Walsh ripped the heart out of England both metaphorically and physically. "
A BBC cricket commentator gets bit gory

Cricket

" He seems to have had a problem with his right
foot, which has run with him all day."
**Could English cricketer Robin Jackman
expect anything else with someone's foot?**

" In Australia we have a word to describe their
[Pakistan's] way of playing cricket: laissez-faire."
**An Aussie TV commentator speaks
for all francophones Down Under**

With his lovely soft hands he just tossed it off.
**Bobby Simpson observes strange goings-on
at a Durham v. Lancashire match**

" They're very experienced Test players with
a lot of caps under them."
**Former England cricket coach Duncan
Fletcher found where his players were
hiding their headgear**

Cricket

This is the sort of pitch which literally castrates a bowler.
Is this Trevor Bailey's idea of a "no ball"?

" Strangely, in slow-motion replay, the ball seemed to hang in the air for even longer. "
Cricket commentator and former player David Acfield makes it sound like a scene from *The Matrix*

" You almost run out of expletives for this man's fielding. "
Cricketer-turned-commentator Chris Broad swears by a colleague's abilities

" It's half of one, six a dozen of the other. "
Maybe Talksport commentator Chris Cowdrey's maths will improve

Cricket

" Once again our consistency has been proved
to be inconsistent. "
**Cricket coach and commentator David
Graveney doesn't consistently get it wrong**

It's a difficult catch to take, especially when you're
running away from the ball.
**Is a Sky Sports commentator accusing
a cricketer of cowardice?**

" If we can beat South Africa on Saturday
that would be a great fillip in our cap. "
**Metaphorically speaking, former
England captain Graham Gooch didn't
have it quite right**

" He is like a guardsman; every part of him erect. "
**Was BBC's cricket legend Henry Blofeld
talking about stiff opposition?**

Cricket

" Dean Hadley has left the field with a back injury; more news on that as soon as it breaks. "
Fractured logic from BBC cricket correspondent Pat Murphy

" Zimbabwe have done well, just as it looked as though the horse had left the stable and gone galloping down the road, they managed to put a chain on the door. "
Cricket commentator Peter Baxter rides in with some horsey metaphors

And this game is coming nicely to a climax; like a well-cooked Welsh rabbit.
A BBC Radio 4 commentator gives it plenty of bunny

" Jack Russell may be the artist but Metson showed he's a rhyming couplet of a wicketkeeper. "
A BBC radio cricket report that was pure poetry

Cricket

" It was all so easy for Walsh. All he had to do was drop an arm and there it was, on the ground. "
Cricket commentator Tony Lewis

" He has got perfect control over the ball right up to the minute he lets it go. "
Cricket correspondent Peter Walker

I presented my trousers to the committee; I had nothing to hide.
Hope England cricket captain Mike Atherton kept his boxer shorts on, though

" They've sent Shah in at three. It's a good move, it'll give him time to play himself in before he explodes. "
Commentator Harsha Bhogle

" We decided to put the foot on the pedal
towards the end – and it came off."
English cricketer Paul Collingwood

" That was a good catch from Matsikenyeri,
running away from himself."
A Sky Sports commentator lacking direction

People have to realise we're the only
northern hemisphere team in cricket.
**Paul Collingwood needs reminding that the
West Indies, India, Pakistan, Sri Lanka and
Bangladesh are also in the northern hemisphere**

" I don't think I've ever seen anything quite like that
before – it's the second time it's happened today."
Déjà vu for BBC commentator Brian Johnston

Cricket

" Ah yes, sledging. In the days before microphones on the pitch, we got that blind MP chap up into the commentary box to lip read. "
BBC cricket commentator Brian Johnston swears by the old methods

Jon Lewis is a real Essex boy…
born in Isleworth, Middlesex.
BBC cricket summariser Tony Lewis has a problem with geography

" Defreitas… just in the back of his mind he is wearing a support. "
It's a good job Geoffrey Boycott took up cricket and not anatomy

Cricket

It's the sort of score you expect to see at the Under-9s on the village green.
Ian Botham on Australia's 60 all out at Trent Bridge in 2015

" It's been a perfect day for us. I never dreamed I'd be able to get eight wickets in a spell. My previous best-ever bowling was seven for twelve against Kimbolton School Under-15s. "
Stuart Broad

" It stinks. I got it out of the bag before. It was rancid. "
Brendon McCullum on his test cap before his 100th Test

" Cricket is not a very big sport in prison. "
Allen Stanford

" I could bowl a heap of poo tomorrow. "
Dale Steyn

Cricket

" Spin bowling is like software. If you don't try and upgrade it, you will fall by the wayside. "
Indian spinner Ravi Ashwin

" The only thing that seems to be in common is they've got wood and they've got a grip. "
Barry Richards on the difference between old and new bats

He's still living off the fact that he coached a team that anyone, even my dog Jerry, could have coached to world domination.
Michael Clarke on John Buchanan

" A snick by Jack Hobbs is a sort of disturbance of a cosmic orderliness. "
Neville Cardus

" That's a remarkable catch by Yardley, especially as the ball quite literally rolled along the ground towards him. "
Mike Denness

Formula
One

It is either the petrol fumes or watching the cars go round and round endlessly which makes racing commentators and drivers lose the plot and be so prone to verbal crashes.

" I don't make mistakes. I make prophecies which immediately turn out to be wrong."
Murray Walker

" It's lap 26 of 58, which unless I'm very much mistaken, is half way."
Murray Walker very much mistaken

" We need to get it up. I wish I could still get it up, but anyway."
Bernie Ecclestone on… noise

" Do my eyes deceive me or is Senna's Lotus sounding rough?"
Formula One commentator Murray Walker

Mansell is slowing it down, taking it easy. Oh no, he isn't! It's a lap record.
Murray Walker

Formula One

" The best classroom of all times was about
two car lengths behind Juan Manuel Fangio. "
Stirling Moss

Brundle is driving an absolutely pluperfect race.
Murray Walker is getting tense

" The battle is well and truly on if it wasn't
on before, and it certainly was. "
Murray Walker

" They make a female look low-maintenance
these days, mate. "
**Mark Webber on the complexities of the
modern F1 car**

" The track is like a Tesco car park. "
**Mark Webber not impressed with the new
Valencia circuit**

This day is good for me. You are old now, so hopefully it will be easier for me this year.
Nico Rosberg wishes Lewis Hamilton a happy 30th birthday

" Your luck goes up and down like swings and roundabouts. "
Former world champion James Hunt

" Alain Prost is in a commanding second position. "
Murray Walker

" Jenson [Button] is literally putting his balls on the line going up against Lewis. "
Formula One summarizer David Coulthard

" Sometimes management is pissed off with me because I tell them what's going to happen. "
Niki Lauda

" I drove like a grandma from there to the end."
Felipe Massa

" It's getting dark, but that's partly
because it's starting to get night."
Damon Hill shedding light as a pundit

" In Spa I heard I had signed for £150m for three
years. I was asking where the pen was but nobody
came back to me!"
Sebastian Vettel

The most important thing is that when we put on
our helmets, we are all the same.
Simona de Silvestro, female driver

" We now have exactly the same situation as we had
at the start of the race, only exactly the opposite."
Murray Walker

Formula One

" Red Bull will be really worried about
the blue smoke coming from the back
of Mark Webber."
Martin Brundle

" That's history. I say history because
it happened in the past."
Murray Walker

" I kind of like to have someone looking
up my arse."
Mario Andretti

" Eddie Irvine is the Ian Paisley of Formula One."
Damon Hill

My first priority is to finish above rather than
below the ground.
James Hunt

" Sure, I am one of the biggest stars in Finland. But we don't have that many."
Kimi Raikkonen

How has Formula One changed since my day?
Less girls, more technology.
Jody Scheckter

" If that's not a lap record, I'll eat the hat I don't normally wear."
Murray Walker

" What does it feel like being rammed up the backside by Barrichello?"
Formula One commentator James Allen

" I've just stopped my startwatch."
Murray Walker

> Michael Schumacher would remain a formidable challenge if he was driving a pram.
> **Frank Williams**

" Alboreto has dropped back up to fifth place."
Murray Walker seems to have misplaced a Formula One driver

" I can't imagine what kind of problem Senna has. I imagine it must be some sort of grip problem."
Murray Walker

" The drivers have one foot on the brake, one on the clutch and one on the throttle."
Speed Channel's Bob Varsha pedalling some nonsense

Formula One

" It's basically the same, just darker. "
No change, then, for stock-car racer
Alan Kulwicki on switching Saturday
night racing to Sunday afternoons

" Schumacher virtually pedalling
his Benetton back with his fists. "
According to Murray Walker, the
German F1 driver was adding extra punch

" There are enough Ferraris to eat
a plate of spaghetti. "
Former Grand Prix champion Jackie Stewart

" Ericsson's record is second to none in the
RAC Rally; he's been second three times. "
A Mitsubishi Motors spokesman doesn't
quite get the point

He is shedding buckets of adrenalin in that car.
Murray Walker makes it sound messy

Formula One

" A mediocre season for Nelson Piquet
as he is now known and always has been. "
Murray Walker

Murray Walker: So Bernie [Ecclestone],
in the 17 years since you bought McLaren,
which of your many achievements do you
think was the most memorable?
Bernie Ecclestone: Well, I don't remember buying
McLaren.
**One team was obviously much the
same as another for Walker, because
Ecclestone owned Brabham**

" Thackwell really can metaphorically
coast home now. "
Murray Walker

And now Jacques Laffite is as close
to Surer as Surer is to Laffite.
Murray Walker

" Nigel Mansell is the last person in the race apart from the five in front of him. "
Murray Walker

" Speaking from memory, I don't know how many points Nelson Piquet has. "
Murray Walker

Murray Walker: What's that? There's a body on the track!!!
Co-presenter: Um, I think that that is a piece of bodywork, from someone's car.
Things are not always as they appear

" I don't want to tempt fate but Damon Hill is now only half a lap from his first Grand Prix win and… and… he's slowing down, Damon Hill is slowing down… he's... he's stopped. "
Did Murray Walker put the mockers on Hill?

Formula One

" This is an interesting circuit because it has inclines, and not just up, but down as well. "
The ups and downs of being Murray Walker

" Cruel luck for Alesi, second on the grid. That's the first time he had started from the front row in a Grand Prix, having done so in Canada earlier this year. "
Murray Walker's knowledge is second to none

" And there's the man in the green flag! "
Murray Walker

" You can't see a digital clock because there isn't one. "
Murray Walker

Murray Walker: And look at the flames coming from the back of Berger's McLaren.
Co-presenter: Actually, Murray, they're not flames, it's the safety light.

Formula One

" ...and there's no damage to the car...
except to the car itself. "
Murray Walker contradicts himself

Only a few more laps to go and then the action
will begin, unless this is the action, which it is.
Murray Walker

" Tombay's hopes, which were nil before,
are absolutely zero now. "
Murray Walker gets negative

" The Italian GP at Monaco... "
**Geography's not Murray Walker's
strong point sometimes**

" ...the enthusiastic enthusiasts... "
Grand Prix tautology from Murray Walker

As you can see, visually, with your eyes...
Can Grand Prix viewers see what Murray Walker is getting at?

" Andrea de Cesaris... the man who has won more Grands Prix than anyone else without actually winning one of them. "
A confused Murray Walker

" And we have had five races so far this year, Brazil, Argentina, Imola, Schumacher and Monaco! "
Murray Walker

" And Damon Hill is coming into the pit lane... yes, it's Damon Hill coming into the Williams pit, and Damon Hill in the pit... no, it's Michael Schumacher! "
A case of mistaken identity for Murray Walker

Formula One

" Into lap 53, the penultimate last lap but one. "
Things don't add up for Murray Walker

There are a lot of ifs in Formula One,
in fact IF is Formula One backwards!
Murray Walker

" And that just shows you how important
the car is in Formula One racing. "
Murray Walker is dead right about that

" A battle is developing between them.
I say developing, because it's not yet on. "
Murray Walker gets his crystal ball out

" A sad ending, albeit a happy one. "
Murray Walker

Formula One

" And Edson Arantes di Nascimento,
commonly known to us as Pelé,
hands the award to Damon Hill,
commonly known to us as Damon Hill."
Murray Walker

" And Michael Schumacher is actually in
a very good position. He is in last place."
**Don't think Schumacher would agree
with Murray Walker**

And now, excuse me while I interrupt myself.
Murray Walker

" Are they on a one-stopper? Are they on
a two? And when I say they, who do I mean?
Well, I don't know. It could be anybody."
**One of those confused days for
Murray Walker**

Formula One

" Ralf Schumacher speaking in German for
our English listeners."
**English listeners would have been as
mystified as Eleanor Oldroyd obviously was**

" Even in five years' time, he will still be
four years younger than Damon Hill."
Murray Walker has got it figured...

Fantastic! There are four different
cars filling the first four places.
Murray Walker states the obvious

" He can't decide whether to leave
his visor half open or half closed."
Murray Walker got it half right

I don't know what happened, but there was a major malmisorganisation problem there.
Murray Walker has a "malmisorganisation problem" with his mouth

" I should imagine that the conditions in the cockpit are totally unimaginable. "
Murray Walker uses his imagination

" Either the car is stationary, or it's on the move. "
Murray Walker

" I've no idea what Eddie Irvine's orders are, but he's following them superlatively well. "
Murray Walker

" If the gloves weren't off before, and they were, they sure are now! "
Murray Walker

" Colin had a hard on in practice earlier,
and I bet he wished he had a hard on now."
**No, really, World Superbike racing
commentator Jack Burnicle was talking
about Colin Edwards's tyre choice**

It looks as though this year there will be 17
Grands Prix for the World Championship,
compared with the traditional 17.
Murray Walker should check his notes

" Now he must not go the wrong way round
the circuit, and unless he can spin himself
stationary through 360 degrees I fail to
see how he can avoid doing so."
Murray Walker gets it wrong by degrees

" In 12th and 13th, the two Jaguars
of Eddie Irvine."
Murray Walker is seeing double

Prost can see Mansell in his earphones.
**Murray Walker reckons Alain
had got eyes each side of his head**

" So this being Michael Schumacher's
10th race in his 151st year in F1."
**Murray Walker makes Schumacher
a real veteran driver**

" The boot's on the other Schumacher now!"
Murray Walker

" The lead car is unique, except for
the one behind it, which is identical."
Murray Walker

" There are seven winners of the Monaco
Grand Prix on the starting line today,
and four of them are Michael Schumacher."
**Oh no! Murray Walker's seeing double
double now**

" There's so many celebrities on this grid,
I can hardly see the wood for the trees. "
Martin Brundle

" Veteran BBC commentator Murray Walker
said it was the blackest day for Grand Prix racing
since he had started covering the sport. "
**This BBC Teletext news piece should have
been checked before transmission, it seems**

" Mark Blundell stops with his front
wheels stationary. "
**Murray Walker can sense
a bit of inertia here**

Since I have been here at McLaren, we have never
really had an amazing rear end.
**Lewis Hamilton speaking about his car
– not the cheerleaders in the pit area**

Formula One

" The first four cars are both on the same tyres."
**Murray Walker must have been a bit tyred
himself to broadcast this**

" There's nothing wrong with
the car except that it's on fire."
**Murray Walker fans the flames
of uncertainty**

" This will be Williams's first win
since the last time a Williams won."
Murray Walker

" The gap between the two cars is 0.9 of a second,
which is less than one second."
Murray Walker's got it figured

I wonder if Watson is in the
relaxed state of mind he's in.
Murray Walker

> I make no apologies for their absence.
> I'm sorry they're not here.
> **Murray Walker is sorry for himself**

" This is lap 54. After that, it's 55, 56, 57, 58
and 59. "
You can count on Murray Walker's figures

" The faster he goes, the quicker he'll get to the pits.
The slower he goes, the longer it will take. "
Murray Walker on the principles of speed

" You might not think that's cricket,
and it's not, it's motor racing. "
**Murray Walker thinks we might
be confused about the difference**

> The young Ralf Schumacher has been
> upstaged by the teenager Jenson Button,
> who is 20.

Murray Walker got it a teen-y bit wrong

" He [Damon Hill] doesn't know –
but if anyone knows he would. "

**Don't know what Murray Walker
knows about this**

" Look up there! That's the sky! "

Murray Walker seems surprised

" If McLaren hadn't gone for Jenson (Button),
they'd have gone for someone else. "

There's no fooling Kimi Raikkonen's manager

" You can cut the tension with a cricket stump. "

Formula One commentator Murray Walker

" You don't expect to be at the top of the mountain the day you start climbing. "
Ron Dennis

" Do I look camouflaged? Maybe I need a matching helmet so you can't see me. "
Daniel Ricciardo

" It was a bee's dick off pole, but at least I'm on the front row. "
Mark Webber

It's a fine line between the White House and the Shite House.
Mark Webber

" I do not speak the English so good, but then I speak the driving very well. "
Emerson Fittipaldi

" Nigel Mansell is so brave, but such a moaner. He should have 'He Who Dares Whines' embroidered on his overalls. "
Simon Barnes

" It will be like lying in a bath with your feet on the taps, but not as comfortable. "
David Coulthard on the driving position in the new Williams-Renault car

" There are only two things no man will admit he can't do well: drive a car and make love. "
Stirling Moss

In my sport the quick are too often listed among the dead.
Jackie Stewart

" I always thought records were there to be broken. "
Michael Schumacher

" When I think about greatness I just know Ayrton Senna. He was great. "
Lewis Hamilton

I'm not interested in tweeting, Facebook and whatever this nonsense is.
Bernie Eccleston

" Formula One would be a paradise without the media. "
Kimi Raikkonen

" I am not designed to finish second or third... I am designed to win. "
Ayrton Senna

" I will always have a part of Ferrari beside me; a part of my heart will always be red. "
Michael Schumacher

Rugby
Union

In amongst the rucks and mauls, there are lots of slips and quips that squeeze through the scrum to give us plenty to rake over.

" To play the game you have to play on the edge, but unfortunately he's gone to the edge of the cliff and jumped off it. "
Warren Gatland, British Lions coach, on Dylan Hartley's ban

" Sometimes you have to put your balls on the line. "
Gatland again, on dropping Brian O'Driscoll

Sometimes you are unlucky. Sometimes you get what you deserve. And sometimes you get a kick in the nuts.
Christian Day of Northampton

" Maybe it would help if I was a foot taller, had hair and didn't look like a pit bull. "
Richard Cockerill on self-image

Rugby Union

" As long as my backside is pointing to the ground, Ewen McKenzie will not coach Australia. "
**An Australian rugby union official
clears up any doubt**

" Wales is not an easy country to coach because, basically, the Welsh are lazy. "
Ex-Scotland coach Jim Telfer

" It's only a thumb, I've got another one. "
Ryan Jones

The way to get out of the poo is to fight with people who are prepared to get in the trenches with you.
Brian Smith, London Irish coach

You never want to be that guy who talks it up and then can't back it up, training like Tarzan and playing like Jane.
James Haskell

" Basically I am like a dog – I just run after a ball. "
Chris Ashton

" The journo was as confused as a goldfish with dementia. "
Nick Cummins, Australian player

" Last year we were all sizzle and steak, this year we had a horror start but now we are off like a bride's nightie. "
Nick Cummins

" And there's Gregor Townsend's knee, looking very disappointed. "
Gavin Hastings

Rugby Union

" Watching France at the moment is like watching clowns at the circus. "
Jeremy Guscott

" I don't know where Jonny Wilkinson is.
I do know where he is, he's not there. "
England hooker Brian Moore

" Pardon my French, but I thought we showed massive balls to go out there and play like that. "
Andy Farrell

You can knock seven bells of **** out of each other and have a pint with him afterwards.
Adam Jones on camaraderie

" Scotland may have to go to some dark places, but we'll bring some torches. "
Scott Johnson, coach

Rugby Union

" Personally I wouldn't go there. You must get bored ****less in Newcastle. "
Louis Nicollin, Montpelier owner

" The knee doesn't trouble me when I'm walking, but it's painful when I kneel, like before my bank manager. "
David Leslie

" You don't like to see hookers going down on players like that. "
Murray Mexted

The relationship between the Welsh and the English is based on trust and understanding. They don't trust us and we don't understand them.
Dudley Wood, former RFU Secretary

Rugby is a good occasion for keeping thirty bullies from the centre of the city.
Oscar Wilde

" Rafter again doing much of the unseen work which the crowd relishes so much. "
Rugby commentator Bill McLaren

" The ref's turned a blind ear. "
New Zealand rugby union commentator Murray Mexted

" A lot of these guys have waited a lifetime not to win this. "
Australian rugby union star David Campese

" If you can't take a punch you should play table tennis. "
Pierre Berbizier

Rugby Union

" Hopefully the rain will hold off for both sides. "
England player Lawrence Dallaglio

" I think you enjoy the game more if you don't know the rules. Anyway, you're on the same wavelength as the referees. "
Jonathan Davies

" The main difference between playing League and Union is that now I get my hangovers on Monday instead of Sunday. "
Tom David

Reporter: What of the future for Welsh rugby?
Welsh captain Mike Watkins: Over to the Angel for a lot of pints.

" Scotland were victims of their own failure. "
Gavin Hastings

> There's no such thing as a lack of confidence.
> You either have it or you don't.
> **England rugby international Rob Andrew**

" I am not getting any younger and there are a few other guys in the same situation. "
England's Nick Easter

" If you go out to get revenge on a team, you'll get bit on the arse. "
Ireland player Sean O'Brien

" If I've seen two more competitive players than Armstrong and Van der Westheizen, I've yet to see them. "
An "are they or aren't they?" conundrum for former Scotland rugby union captain and pundit Gavin Hastings

" This lad's a butcher – but I've never
had any of his meat. "
Rugby league commentator Eddie Waring

They've got their heads in the sand.
It's a Canute job.
**A mixed-up rugby union commentator
gets his metaphors in a twist**

" And the blue and white hoops of Sale will
no doubt act as a red flag to the Tigers. "
**Colourful commentary from the BBC's
Ian Brown**

" The ball is often a handicap in these conditions. "
**Former rugby player and commentator Nigel
Starmer-Smith finds his tongue a handicap, too**

…and, in contrast, we have the New Zealand team littered with internationals.
The BBC commentator has no surprises for the Kiwis

" Nigel Starmer-Smith had seven craps for England some years ago. "
Presenter and pundit Jimmy Hill

" Knowledge is knowing that a tomato is a fruit; wisdom is knowing not to put it in a fruit salad. "
Ireland's Brian O'Driscoll's hard-to-fathom answer when asked what it was like to play with fellow British and Irish Lion Martin Johnson

" Condom is back in French pack. "
Was this rugby union headline in *the Independent* newspaper in French letters?

Rugby Union

" The French selectors never do anything by halves; for the first international of the season against Ireland they dropped half the three-quarter line. "
Give Nigel Starmer-Smith half a chance and he'll get it wrong

" We go to the four corners of the globe to bring you the best of rugby league – Batley, Oldham, Wigan and France. "
Geography lesson needed for commentator Eddie Hemmings

" We all know England are the best rugby team in the world and next weekend, when they play Scotland, we'll find out if they are the best in Britain. "
Lord Archer obviously rates Britain highly

We are committing our own suicide.
Suicide is so personal for Scotland rugby union team coach Ian McGeechan

They're a bit laxative.
**Rugby league's Robbie Paul is a bit
lackadaisical with words**

" Andrew Mehrtens loves it when
Daryl Gibson comes inside of him. "
**New Zealand rugby commentator's
vocal slip-up**

"…and Dusty Hare kicked 19 of the 17 points. "
**David Coleman covers rugby for a change and
struggles with the scoring system**

" Frustration was the buzzword in the
squad on Saturday. "
Former England coach Martin Johnson

" We have self-belief in each other. "
A very believable Gavin Hastings

" And he's got the icepack on his groin there,
so possibly not the old shoulder injury."
**That medical degree came in handy
for commentator Ray French**

" I don't like this new law, because your first instinct
when you see a man on the ground is to go down
on him."
Murray Mexted

He's looking for some meaningful
penetration into the backline.
...and again...

" Everybody knows that I have
been pumping Martin Leslie for
a couple of seasons now."
Another Murray Mexted classic

I just love it when Mehrtens
comes on the inside of Marshall.
Murray Mexted can't stop himself

" I'm just gutted, gutted for all the fans and
everyone at home. I'm sorry we let everyone
down. "
**Stuart Lancaster, England head coach, after
being knocked out of the 2015 World Cup**

" Mike may be a bit upset and that's fine. What did
he say? That I missed my mum? Who doesn't miss
their mum? "
Sam Burgess, proving he's just a mummy's boy

" I went to Mass this morning and even the priest
came out and put his hands up in the air to
celebrate. "
**Shaun Edwards after Wales's victory over
England in the 2015 World Cup**

" Yes, it's a very humbling part of the game. You can dominate one day and get your pants pulled down on another. "
Michael Cheika, Australian head coach

" We play a similar style of rugby to England but we have better-looking players. "
South African hooker Schalk Brits

We are going to bash each other for 80 minutes and then enjoy a good chat and maybe a beer afterwards.
South Africa's Duane Vermeulen

" A talent hits a target no one can hit, but a genius hits a target no one else can see. "
Johan van Graan, South Africa's assistant coach

It is like kissing your sister.
South African coach Heyneke Meyer's view on third-place final

" We talked about what we wanted to do at half-time. It must have been a terrible speech. "
Canada coach Kieran Crowley

" I had breakfast with my wife for the first time in a long time. At least I still think she's my wife, I don't know if she still thinks I'm her husband. "
Eddie Jones, then Japan coach, after their World Cup exit

Tennis

There have been some smashing moments from tennis players and commentators across the ages and here we serve up some real aces.

" I did play well in Australia. I don't know where you were. Were you under a rock? "
Roger Federer questioning a journalist

" The Gullikson twins here. An interesting pair, both from Wisconsin. "
Dan Maskell

Sure, I've been on the tube – I caught it to Eastbourne once.
Serena Williams

" As Boris Becker sits there, his eyes staring out in front of him, I wonder what he's thinking. I think he's thinking, 'I am Boris Becker.' At least I hope that's what he's thinking. "
BBC tennis commentator John Barrett

" Lleyton Hewitt… his two greatest strengths are his legs, his speed, his agility and his competitiveness."
Pat Cash doubles up

" Obviously, like Wembley is synonymous with tennis, snooker is synonymous with Sheffield."
Richard Caborn, former Minister of Sport

" When Martina is tense it helps her relax."
Dan Maskell

" Laura Robson… solid between the ears."
Virginia Wade

She changed coaches more times than I changed wives.
The many times married Nick Bollettieri on Laura Robson

Tennis

" The only thing that could have stopped Nadal this year is his knees. "
Chris Wilkinson

" Nothing can prepare me for this. I just hope I play well and don't poop my pants. "
Blaz Rola on facing Andy Murray

" It sucks. "
Heather Watson unimpressed by her performance at the Australian Open

" Federer is human, but for how long? "
BBC tennis commentator

Martina, she's got several layers of steel out there, like a cat with nine lives.
Wimbledon champion and BBC tennis commentator Virginia Wade

Tennis

" That shot he has to obliterate from
his mind a little bit."
Mark Cox

" If someone says I'm not feminine, I say 'screw it'."
Rosie Casals

I call tennis the McDonald's of sport – you go in,
they make a quick buck out of you, and you're out.
Pat Cash

" I still break racquets, but now I do it
in a positive way."
Goran Ivanisevic

" Nobody likes me. And I couldn't care
a goddam stuff."
Jimmy Connors

" Getting your first serve in is a great way to avoid double faults. "
Former Australian tennis player John Fitzgerald

" It's quite clear that Virginia Wade is thriving on the pressure now that the pressure on her to do well is off. "
Harry Carpenter

The trouble with me is that every match I play against five opponents: umpire, crowd, ball boys, court and myself.
Goran Ivanisevic on his unequal struggle

" Whoever said, 'It's not whether you win or lose that counts,' probably lost. "
Martina Navratilova

Tennis

Time to remove every item of clothing and run through the streets of Glasgow.
Andy Murray gets swept away with Jamie Ward's Davis Cup victory

" I can cry like Roger, it's just a shame I can't play like him. "
Andy Murray

" It'll certainly give the pigeons something to do. "
Pat Cash on unveiling his own bust

" He can't cook. "
Michael Chang on Pete Sampras's weaknesses

" I threw the kitchen sink at him but he went to the bathroom and got his tub. "
Andy Roddick on losing to Roger Federer

And here's Zivojinovic, six feet six inches tall and 14 pounds 10 ounces.
BBC tennis commentator Dan Maskell makes light of the player

" Billie Jean King, with the look on her face that says she can't believe it... because she never believes it, and yet, somehow, I think she does."
Unbelievable comments from BBC tennis pundit Max Robertson

" I'm an American. You can't go on where you were born. If you do, then John McEnroe would be a German."
Pundit and tennis legend Martina Navratilova misplaces Mac's heritage

" Miss Stove seems to be going off the boil."
Tennis commentator Peter West likes a pun

Tennis

" You can always feel much better if someone
endorses the call – even if they are wrong. "
Virginia Wade

Sampras's heart must have been in his hands.
**I've heard of wearing your heart on your
sleeve but this Sky commentator sees more**

" I wonder if the Germans have a
word for *Blitzkrieg* in their language. "
***Achtung!* A language gaffe from
South African tennis pundit Frew McMillan**

" Nobody is blaming the linesman.
Of course, he did make a couple
of big mistakes. Really big ones. "
**Tennis star Marat Saffin makes
his point on officialdom**

Tennis

" I have a feeling that, if she had been playing herself, she would have won that point. "
Former Australian tennis player and commentator Bob Hewitt

Martina Hingis is going through a part of her life which she has never been through before.
BBC tennis commentator

" If you can't get near a radio, Henman's taken the first set. "
A bit of radio ga-ga from BBC Radio

" Sampras, in white, serves with his baggy shorts. "
The BBC's Ian Carter has a theory about why Pete's balls were nearly always in

" These ball boys are marvellous. You don't even notice them. There's a left-handed one over there. I noticed him earlier. "
Max Robertson

Tennis

" She never loses a match. If she loses a match,
it's because her opponent beats her."
Former tennis player and commentator
Pam Shriver seemed a little confused

" She comes from a tennis-playing family.
Her father's a dentist."
BBC commentator

" Well, judging from his serves, Larsson
will either win this match or lose it."
A Eurosport commentator was definitely
hedging his bets

Tennis is one of those games like all other games.
Wimbledon champion Virginia Wade doesn't
think tennis is unique

Tennis

" I haven't [met him] yet but I have long been an admirer of his hair. Great hair. "
Andy Roddick on David Beckham

" I believe this bird came all the way from Belgrade to help me. "
Novak Djokovic on that little extra help

" Actually I am a tri-citizen. I've got a Hungarian passport as well. Just add that into the mix, guys. I mean, I'm pretty much the female version of Jason Bourne. "
Johanna Konta, the new star of "British" tennis

" I'm good from behind. "
Daria Gavrilova

I named one of my dogs after him. He was someone I loved growing up.
Andy Murray on boyhood idol Lleyton Hewitt

Tennis

" As much as I would like to be a robot, I'm not. "
Serena Williams

" Victory is fleeting. Losing is forever. "
Billie Jean King

Good shot, bad luck and hell are the five basic
words to be used in a game of tennis.
Virginia Wade

" At Wimbledon, the ladies are simply the candles
on the cake. "
John Newcombe

" I may have exaggerated a bit when I said that 80%
of the top 100 women tennis players are fat pigs.
What I meant to say was 75% of the top 100
women are fat pigs. "
Richard Krajicek

American
Football

The focus may be on getting those crucial ten yards on the pitch but the battle to win the war of words is just as intense.

" My gluteus maximus is hurteus enormous."
Tony Campbell

My sister's expecting a baby, and I don't know if
I'm going to be an uncle or an aunt.
North Carolina State player Chuck Nevitt

" He treats us like men. He lets us wear earrings."
Houston's Torrin Polk is so grateful to his coach

" A tie is like kissing your sister."
Duffy Daugherty

" Coach Lombardi is very fair. He treats us all like
dogs."
Packers legend Henry Jordan

" If winning isn't everything, why do they keep
score?"
Vince Lombardi

" Does Tom Landry smile? I don't know.
I only played there nine years. "
Walt Garrison

" I resigned as coach because of illness and fatigue.
The fans were sick and tired of me. "
John Ralston, Denver Broncos

" Most football players are temperamental.
That's 90% temper and 10% mental. "
Doug Plank

On this team, we were all united in a
common goal: to keep my job.
Lou Holtz, coach

" I've been big ever since I was little. "
William "The Refrigerator" Perry

What's the difference between a three-week-old puppy and a sportswriter? In six weeks, the puppy stops whining.
Mike Ditka, football coach

" The NFL, like life, is full of idiots. "
Randy Cross

" Defensively, I think it's important for us to tackle. "
Karl Mecklenburg

" The man who complains about the way the ball bounces is likely the one who dropped it. "
Lou Holtz

" Hey, the offensive linemen are the biggest guys on the field, they're bigger than everybody else, and that's what makes them the biggest guys on the field. "
John Madden

American Football

" I have two weapons; my arms, my legs
and my brain. "
Michael Vick

" Sure, luck means a lot in football. Not having
a good quarterback is bad luck. "
Don Shula

" I'm not allowed to comment on lousy officiating. "
Jim Finks

I dunno. I never smoked any Astroturf.
**Joe Namath after being asked if he preferred
grass or Astroturf**

" If I drop dead tomorrow, at least I'll know I died
in good health. "
Bum Phillips

" I want to rush for 1,000 or 1,500 yards.
Whichever comes first. "
Running back George Rogers

" I never graduated college, but I was only there for
two terms – Truman's and Eisenhower's. "
Alex Karras

Emotion is highly overrated in football. My wife
Corky is emotional as hell but can't play football
worth a damn.
John McKay

" If my mother put on a helmet and shoulder pads
and a uniform that wasn't the same as the one I
was wearing, I'd run over her if she was in my
way. And I love my mother. "
Bo Jackson

American Football

" I may be dumb, but I'm not stupid. "
Terry Bradshaw

" Nobody in football should be called a genius.
A genius is a guy like Norman Einstein. "
Joe Theismann

" People say I'll be drafted in the first round,
maybe even higher. "
Craig Heyward

" After being pelted with oranges at the Orange
Bowl game – I'm glad we're not going to the Gator
Bowl. "
Lou Holtz, former college player and coach

If a nuclear bomb is ever dropped on the United
States, the only things that will survive are
Astroturf and coach Don Shula.
Charles "Bubba" Smith

American Football

" Football isn't a contact sport, it's a collision sport. Dancing is a contact sport. "
Duffy Daugherty

" Football kickers are like taxi cabs. You can always go out and hire another one. "
Buddy Ryan

" The only qualifications for a lineman are to be big and dumb. To be a back, you only have to be dumb. "
Knute Rockne

As a college player at Princeton, I always felt like Dolly Parton's shoulder straps. I knew I had a job to do, but felt totally incapable of doing it.
Actor James Stewart

" If you aren't going all the way, why go at all?"
Joe Namath

" You're never a loser until you quit trying."
Mike Ditka

It's not whether you get knocked down; it's whether you get up.
Vince Lombardi

" Today I will do what others won't, so tomorrow I can accomplish what others can't."
Jerry Rice

" Rapport? You mean like, 'You run as fast as you can, and I'll throw it as far as I can?'"
Jeff Kemp, 49ers football quarterback, simplifies his relationship with wide receiver Jerry Rice

Baseball

Here are a few "strikes", the odd home run and an occasional curveball as we try to cover all the bases.

Baseball

" I was thinking of making a comeback until I pulled a muscle vacuuming."
Johnny Bench

" It ain't the heat, it's the humility."
Yogi Berra

" When we [England] have a World Series, we ask other countries to participate."
John Cleese

I watch a lot of baseball on the radio.
Gerald Ford, former US President

" Crowd? This isn't a crowd. It's a focus group!"
Fran Healy on a disappointing turnout

" Always go to other people's funerals; otherwise they won't go to yours."
Yogi Berra

> Baseball is 90 per cent mental. The other half is physical.
> **Yogi Berra has a maths problem**

" I was glad to see Italy win. All the guys on the team were Italians."
Former Dodgers manager Tom Lasorda

" This is like deja vu all over again."
Former New York Yankees player Yogi Berra

" Predictions are difficult. Especially about the future."
Yogi Berra

" Any pitcher who throws at a batter and deliberately tries to hit him is a communist."
Alvin Dark

" Philadelphia fans would boo a funeral."
Bo Belinsky

" I never questioned the integrity of an umpire.
Their eyesight, yes."
Leo Durocher

" What have they lost, nine of their last eight?"
Ted Turner

He must have made that before he died.
Yogi Berra referring to a Steve McQueen movie

" I take a two-hour nap, from one o'clock to four."
Yogi Berra

" After I hit a home run I had a habit of running
the bases with my head down. I figured the pitcher
already felt bad enough without me showing him
up rounding the bases."
Mickey Mantle

" I gave [pitcher] Mike Cuellar more chances
than I gave my first wife. "
Baltimore Orioles manager Earl Weaver

" They say some of my stars drink whiskey. But
I have found that the ones who drink milkshakes
don't win many ballgames. "
Casey Stengel

" Out of what – a thousand? "
**Mickey Rivers on hearing his Yankees
teammate Reggie Jackson has an IQ of 165**

" Just give me 25 guys on the last year of their
contracts; I'll win a pennant every year. "
Sparky Anderson

People think we make $3 million or $4 million
a year. They don't realize that most of us
only make $500,000.
Pete Incaviglia

" I walk into the clubhouse today and it's like walking into the Mayo Clinic. We have four doctors, three therapists and five trainers. Back when I broke in, we had one trainer who carried a bottle of rubbing alcohol, and by the 7th inning he'd already drunk it. "
Tommy Lasorda

When you get that nice celebration coming into the dugout and you're getting your ass hammered by guys – there's no better feeling than to have that done.
Matt Stairs

" Two hours is about as long as any American can wait for the close of a baseball game... or anything else for that matter. "
Albert Spalding

He's got power enough to hit home-runs
in any park, including Yellowstone.
Sparky Anderson on Willie Stargell

" Don't call 'em dogs. Dogs are loyal and they run
after balls. "
**St. Louis Browns manager Luke Sewell
responding to criticism of his team**

" There's a thin line between genius and insanity,
and in Larry's case it was so thin you could see
him drifting back and forth across it. "
Brooklyn Dodgers manager Leo Durocher

" Just take the ball and throw it where you want to.
Throw strikes. Home plate don't move. "
Leroy "Satchel" Paige

" One night we play like King Kong, the next night
like Fay Wray. "
Terry Kennedy, on the San Diego Padres

Things were so bad in Chicago last summer that by the 5th inning the White Sox were selling hot dogs to go.
Ken Brett

" Baseball without fans is like Jayne Mansfield without a sweater. Hang on, that can be taken two ways. "
Richard Nixon

" When Athletics' owner Charlie Finley had his heart operation, it took eight hours – seven and a half to find his heart. "
Steve McCatt

" Baseball is the favourite American sport because it's so slow. Any idiot can follow it. And just about any idiot can play it. "
Gore Vidal

" I have just one superstition. Whenever I hit a home run, I make certain I touch all four bases. "
Babe Ruth

Baseball

" I don't think I can be expected to take seriously a game which takes less than three days to complete. "
Tom Stoppard

In a way, an umpire is like a woman. He makes quick decisions, never reverses them, and doesn't think you're safe when you're out.
Larry Goatz

" The doctors X-rayed my head and found nothing. "
Baseball legend Dizzy Dean

" When you come to a fork in the road, take it! "
Baseball's Yogi Berra speaks with forked tongue

" Rich Folkers is throwing up in the bullpen. "
Former baseball player and commentator Jerry Coleman thinks he might be sick of baseball

Basketball

Players and coaches go through hoops to gain supremacy over each other when they are busy point scoring off court.

Basketball

" We don't need referees in basketball, but
it gives the white guys something to do. "
Charles Barkley

" When I die, I want to come back as me. "
Mark Cuban

" I'm often mentioned in the same sentence as
Michael Jordan. You know 'That Scott Hastings,
he's no Michael Jordan'. "
The self-deprecating Scott Hastings

" Billy Tubbs is what's known as a contact
coach – all con and no tact. "
Bob Reinhardt

We were so bad last year that the cheerleaders
stayed home and phoned in their cheers.
Pat Williams

Basketball

" The game is my wife. It demands loyalty and responsibility and it gives me back fulfilment and peace. "
Michael Jordan

Reporter: Did you visit the Parthenon while in Greece?
Basketball star Shaquille O'Neal: I can't really remember the names of all the clubs we went to.

" I told him, 'Son, what is it with you. Is it ignorance or apathy?' He said, 'Coach, I don't know and I don't care.' "
Utah Jazz president Frank Layden

" Left hand, right hand, it doesn't matter. I'm amphibious. "
Basketball player Charles Shackleford

Basketball

" I've never lost a game. I just ran out of time."
Michael Jordan

There are really only two plays: *Romeo and Juliet*,
and put the darn ball in the basket.
Abe Lemons

" The season is too long, the game is too long
and the players are too long."
Jack Dolph

" We can't win at home. We can't win on the road.
As general manager, I just can't figure out where
else to play."
Pat Williams

" Fans never fall asleep at our games, because they're
afraid they might get hit by a pass."
George Raveling

Basketball

" In my prime I could have handled Michael Jordan. Of course, he would be only 12 years old. "
Jerry Sloan

" You don't hesitate with Michael, or you'll end up on some poster in a gift shop someplace. "
Fatten Spencer

Mick Jagger is in better shape than far too many NBA players. It's up in the air whether the same can be said of Keith Richards.
Bill Walton

" I only know how to play two ways: reckless and abandon. "
Earvin "Magic" Johnson

" These are my new shoes. They're good shoes. They won't make you rich like me, they won't make you rebound like me, they definitely won't make you handsome like me. They'll only make you have shoes like me. That's it."
Charles Barkley

" It's almost like we have ESPN."
Earvin "Magic" Johnson on his telepathic understanding with James Worthy

If you make every game a life and death proposition, you're going to have problems. For one thing, you'll be dead a lot.
Dean Smith

" Any time Detroit scores more than 100 points and holds the other team below 100 points, they almost always win."
Doug Collins

Basketball

Nobody roots for Goliath.
Wilt Chamberlain

" We have a great bunch of outside shooters.
Unfortunately, all our games are played indoors. "
Weldon Drew

" We're going to turn this team around
360 degrees. "
Jason Kidd

" I heard Tonya Harding is calling herself the Charles
Barkley of figure skating. I was going to sue her for
defamation of character, but then I realised I have
no character. "
The self-deprecating Charles Barkley

" I believe in higher education. You know 6'8", 6'9", 6'10".
David Games

The way defences are operating these days, the other team starts picking you up when you walk out of the hotel lobby.
Doc Hayes

" The way to stop Kareem Abdul-Jabbar is to get real close to him and breathe on his goggles."
John Kerr

" I can accept failure, everyone fails at something. But I can't accept not trying."
Michael Jordan

Basketball

He dribbles a lot and the opposition doesn't like it. In fact you can see it all over their faces.
A performance that had an NBC analyst salivating

" I've never had major knee surgery on any other part of my body. "
NBA star Winston Bennett

" He has the players too happy. "
Boston Celtics' general manager Red Auerbach is critical of Bill Russell's coaching

Ice Hockey

For a sport that is known for its speed and brutality, surprisingly some of the more vicious moments come when the teams are off the ice.

Ice Hockey

" All hockey players are bi-lingual: they speak English and profanity."
Gordie Howe

" Hockey is the only game that can be played equally well with the lights out."
Jim Murray

A fast body-contact game played by men with clubs in their hands and knives laced to their feet.
Paul Gallico

" Goaltending is a normal job, sure. How would you like it in your job if every time you made a small mistake, a red light went on over your desk and 15,000 people stood up and yelled at you?"
Jacques Plante

Ice Hockey

" Red ice sells hockey tickets. "
Bob Stewart

If you've only got one day to live,
come see the Toronto Maple Leafs.
It'll seem like forever.
Pat Foley

" I went to a fight the other night and
a hockey game broke out. "
Rodney Dangerfield

" By the age of 18, the average American
has witnessed 200,000 acts of violence on
television, most of them occurring during
Game 1 of the NHL playoff series. "
Sportswriter Steve Rushin

Ice Hockey

Half the game is mental; the other half
is being mental.
Jim McKenny

" Hockey is the only job I know where you get paid
to have a nap on the day of the game. "
Chico Resch

" Ice hockey is a form of disorderly conduct in
which the score is kept. "
Doug Larson

" I know my players don't like my practices, but
that's OK because I don't like their games. "
Harry Neale

" I think he knows all my tricks. Or the fact
I don't have any tricks. "
Brendan Shanahan

Ice Hockey

" They say you're not a coach in the league till you've been fired. I must be getting pretty good. "
Terry Simpson

" Every day you guys look worse and worse. And today you played like tomorrow. "
John Mariucci to his US Olympic team

" I don't like hockey. I'm just good at it. "
Brett Hull

I don't have nightmares about my team. You gotta sleep before you have nightmares.
Bep Guidolin, Kansas City Scouts coach

" Why is a puck called a puck? Because 'dirty little bastard' was already taken. "
Devils goalie Martin Brodeur

" Some guys play hockey. Gretzky plays 40mph chess. "
Lowell Cohn, sportswriter

I slept like a baby. Every two hours, I woke up and cried.
Tom McVie, coach

" Sometimes people ask, 'Are hockey fights real?' I say, 'If they weren't, I'd get in more of them.' "
Wayne Gretzky

" The three most important elements in hockey are: the forecheck, the backcheck and the paycheck. "
Sabres' Gilbert Perreault

" The playoffs separate the men from the boys, and we found out we have a lot of boys in our dressing room. "
Neil Smith, NY Rangers General Manager

The only difference between this and Custer's last stand was that Custer didn't have to look at the tape afterwards.
Terry Crisp, Tampa Bay Lightning coach, after a 10–0 thrashing

" You miss 100% of the shots that you don't take. "
Wayne Gretzky

Snooker

Down the years snooker has provided
plenty of potty-mouthed moments
and more than enough colourful
confrontation on the baize as
well as off it.

" I'm up and down like a whore's drawers. "
**Ronnie O' Sullivan makes a
colourful comparison**

Jimmy White has popped out to the toilet to
compose himself before the final push.
Steve Davis getting a bit too close for comfort

" And Griffiths has looked at that blue four times
now, and it still hasn't moved. "
Ted Lowe

" I always have to drink six pints before I'm able to
start playing properly. "
Bill Werbeniuk's meticulous preparation

" I like playing in Sheffield, it's full of
melancholy, happy-go-lucky people. "
Alex Higgins

Snooker

" I'll tell you what I would like to do
to Davis. I'd like to stick his cue…"
Alex Higgins

" The audience are literally electrified
and glued to their seats."
Snooker commentator Ted Lowe

" Frankly, I would rather have a drink
with Idi Amin."
Alex Higgins on Steve Davis

This looks like being the longest frame
in the match, even though it's the first.
Clive Everton

" Oh, that's a brilliant shot. The odd thing
is his mum's not very keen on snooker."
Snooker commentator Ted Lowe

Snooker

" All the reds are in the open apart from the blue."
John Virgo

" Tony Meo is eyeing up a plant."
David Vine

" I don't think it's clever to retire at the top.
I think it's best to go out screaming."
Steve Davis

" 99 times out of 1,000 he would
have potted that ball."
Snooker commentator Ted Lowe

From this position you've got to fancy either
yourself or your opponent winning.
**Former snooker player and commentator
Kirk Stevens**

Snooker

" If I had to make the choice between
staying married and playing snooker,
snooker would win. "
Ray Reardon

I've always said the difference between
winning and losing is nothing at all.
**Former snooker player and
commentator Terry Griffiths**

" Suddenly Alex Higgins is 7–0 down. "
Snooker commentator David Vine

" I don't know if I'm still The Rocket
– perhaps I'm more like Thomas the
Tank Engine these days. "
Ronnie O'Sullivan

" That's inches away from being millimetre perfect. "
Snooker commentator Ted Lowe

Snooker

" He's lucky in one sense and lucky in the other. "
Ted Lowe

" What Graeme Dott likes to do is win frames. "
Snooker's Steve Davis

" [Alex] Higgins first entered the championship
10 years ago. That was for the first time,
of course. "
Ted Lowe chalks up a definite first

" And it is my guess that Steve Davis will try to
score as many points as he can in this frame. "
**Ted Lowe has at least got the point of
snooker nailed down**

Steve Davis has a tough consignment in
front of him.
Ted Lowe

Snooker

A little pale in the face, but then his name
is White.
Is Ted Lowe a little red-faced over this comment?

" That pot puts the game beyond reproach. "
Ted Lowe goes in for the blame game

" All square, all the way round. "
Ted Lowe squares the circle

" There is, I believe, a time limit for playing a shot.
But I think it's true to say that nobody knows
what the limit is. "
Ted Lowe needs a rule book

" Jimmy White has that wonderful gift of being
able to point his cue where he is looking. "
**Ted Lowe reckons there's no room for cross-
eyed snooker players, then?**

Snooker

When you start off, it's usually nil-nil.
Former snooker champion Steve Davis

" Just enough points here for Tony
to pull the cat out of the fire. "
**Can TV snooker commentator Ray Edmonds
smell burning fur somewhere?**

" Tony Meo is beginning to find his potting boots. "
**Former player and snooker commentator
Rex Williams**

" The match has gradually and suddenly
come to a climax. "
David Vine isn't too sure about this, though

" No one came closer to winning the
title last year than the runner-up. "
**Former snooker player and commentator
Dennis Taylor**

" Valour was the better part of discretion there. "
**TV snooker commentator Jack Karnehm
mixes his metaphors**

" Sometimes the deciding frame is
always the hardest one to win. "
Dennis Taylor

" That said, the inevitable failed to happen. "
**TV snooker commentator John Pulman
was inevitably wrong about that**

" 10–4 and that could mean exactly what it means. "
Well, David Vine knows what HE means

And now for some snooker news: Steve Davis has
crashed out of the UK Billiards Championship.
**Snooker player and commentator Allan Taylor
gets his green baize sports mixed up**

Snooker

" Ray Reardon is one of the great Crucible champions. He won it five times when the championship was played away from the Crucible. "
David Vine misses his own point

" And that's the third time this session he's missed his waistcoat pocket with the chalk. "
Eagle-eyed Ted Lowe

" There are those with commentators' eyes, and then there's Willie Thorne. "
John Virgo

Steve is going for the pink ball – and for those of you who are watching in black and white, the pink is next to the green.
Colourful commentary from Ted Lowe

Snooker

" Jimmy White is known as 'The Nearly Man'
of snooker, but a lot of people forget that
he's got the second best record in the world
championship in the 1990s. "
**Does snooker ace Steve Davis reckon
White is second to none?**

This is where the precision has to be precise.
**Former snooker player John Spencer
knows precisely**

" At certain times here, and even in the hotel,
there's nearly a stench of death in the place. "
**Snooker is life and death for Irish star
Fergal O'Brien**

" For those of you watching who do not have
TV sets, live commentary is on Radio 2. "
Ted Lowe mystifies viewers and listeners

Snooker

" Fred Davis, the doyen of snooker. Now 67 years of age and too old to get his leg over, prefers to use his left hand. "
Commentator Ted Lowe was referring to snooker, of course

" If you get to 9-7... you start seeing alarm bells then. "
Commentator John Parrott

It's all about the length and this one doesn't look hard enough to me.
Is John Virgo being rude?

" Unbelievable. Winner, winner chicken dinner. "
Stuart Bingham, on winning snooker's World Championship

Snooker

Whoever called snooker "chess with balls" was rude, but right.
Clive James

" The relentless pursuit of perfection has been my problem over the years. It's maybe held me back. "
Ronnie O'Sullivan

" He's completely disappeared. He's gone back to his dressing room, nobody knows where he has gone. "
Ted Lowe

Horse Racing

Confusion in the heat of the moment as a race reaches its climax or uncertainty about whether they are referring to the horse or the rider, these are the obstacles faced by race commentators and pundits. Throw in such words as "hard", "soft" and "ride" and you can see why some have the occasional verbal fall.

Horse Racing

" She ran through the field like water through a duck. "
What sport was former jockey and TV presenter John Francombe watching?

" Well, you gave the horse a wonderful ride – everybody saw that. "
Television presenter Des Lynam

" Princess Anne's horse is literally eating up the ground. "
A new diet for horse-racing correspondent Peter Bromley

This is really a lovely horse.
I once rode her mother.
Racing commentator Ted Walsh

Horse Racing

" …and there's the unmistakable figure
of Joe Mercer… or is it Lester Piggott?"
**Maybe horse-racing correspondent
Brough Scott needed glasses?**

" Tony has a quick look between
his legs and likes what he sees."
***Winning Post*'s Stewart Machin
speaks for all men**

The racecourse is as level as a billiard ball.
**A verbal balls-up here from Channel 4
horse-racing man John Francombe**

" My word! Look at that magnificent erection."
**You would never have guessed that Brough
Scott was talking about the new stand at
Doncaster racecourse**

Horse Racing

" They usually have four or five dreams a night about coming from different positions. "
Former champion rider Willie Carson telling the BBC's Clare Balding how jockeys prepare for a big race

" A jockey without a whip is like a carpenter without a spanner. "
Frankie Dettori obviously wasn't a carpenter before he became a top jockey

He was going all right until he fell.
Jockey John Cullen

" This is the first time she has had 14 hands between her legs. "
John Francombe

A lot of horses get distracted. It's just human nature.
Horse trainer Nick Zito

" In this yard, all horses are treated equally, but there is one animal that knows he's a little more equal than the others. "
Equality comes unequally in a BBC News item about star horse Kauto Star

" The bookies are literally waltzing out of here under cloud nine. "
Commentator Colm Murray at the Cheltenham Festival

" At Ascot today the heat is quite hot. "
BBC presenter Judith Chalmers at a flat-racing event

It looks as though that premature excitement may have been premature.
BBC racing man Brough Scott

" That's the magic of TV, I've just heard over the headphones that Noalto was third."
Technology has been a mystery for the BBC's David Coleman.

" A volcano trapped inside an iceberg."
Hugh McIlvanney on Lester Piggott

" It is surely the epitome of pointlessness to gamble within your limits."
Clement Freud

" Premature ejockulation."
Clare Balding on the unseating of a jockey

Horse Racing

" Horses don't answer back. "
**Mick Channon on choosing racehorse training
over football-club management**

" Horses will break your bones, your bank and your
heart. "
Writer Simon Barnes

" Get the ****in' bubbly open. "
Frankie Dettori after winning the Derby

" If you lose, you're concrete – if you win, you can
have Belinda for the night. "
East End horse owner to jockey

All my good horses have had good heads, their
eyes wide apart. Do you trust a human when their
eyes are too close together?
Henry Cecil

Selecting a horse is like finding a girlfriend – you have to love them at first sight because you're seeing them at 6.30 every morning.
Ben Pollock, trainer

" Lochsong – she's like Linford Christie… without the lunchbox. "
Frankie Dettori

" The horse sadly died this morning, so it looks like he won't be running in the Gold Cup. "
Charlie McCann, trainer

" They are unpredictable – horses are like women. "
Jimmy Pike, jockey

Horse Racing

Brough Scott: What are your immediate thoughts, Walter?

Walter Swinburn: I don't have any immediate thoughts at the moment.

Other
Sports

A mixture of mishaps, muck-ups and madness from the saddle and the oche … in boats and on dry land, here is a miscellany of mischief.

Other Sports

" And he's out there in front breaking wind
for the rest of the peloton. "
Phil Liggett on cycling strategy

Cycling is such a stupid sport. Next time
you are in a car travelling at 40 mph
think about jumping out – naked.
That's what it's like when we crash.
David Millar

" There are two chairs that will kill you
– the electric chair and the armchair. "
**Former showjumping champion
Harvey Smith on the dangers of retirement**

" There are, they say, fools, bloody fools
and men that remount in a steeplechase. "
John Oaksey

Other Sports

" He's been burning the midnight oil at both ends. "
Darts commentator Sid Waddell

" Only one word for it – magic darts. "
Darts commentator Tony Green

I can't tell who's leading. It's either Oxford or Cambridge.
John Snagge on the Oxford and Cambridge Boat Race

" Teddy McCarthy to John McCarthy, no relation, John McCarthy back to Teddy McCarthy, still no relation... "
Gaelic football commentator Micheal O'Muircheartaigh

" I had him by the bollocks but
I just didn't squeeze. "
Phil Taylor

" I thought Aidy was rubbish, and my
rubbish was just a bit better than his. "
Gary Anderson, darts player

" The atmosphere is so tense, if Elvis walked in
with a portion of chips, you could hear the
vinegar sizzle on them. "
Sid Waddell

And this is Gregorieva from Bulgaria. I saw
her snatch this morning and it was amazing!
Weightlifting commentator Pat Glenn

Ah, isn't that nice, the wife of the Cambridge president is hugging the cox of the Oxford crew.
BBC Boat Race commentator

" All I had to do is keep turning left! "
George Robson, winner of the 1946 Indy 500

" You win some, you lose some,
you wreck some. "
Dale Earnhardt Snr

" I feel safer on a racetrack than I do on Houston's freeways. "
AJ Foyt

In cycling you can put all your money on one horse.
Cycling legend Stephen Roche changes saddles

" This seesaw's going up and down like a roundabout, what a match!"
Sid Waddell

" What a man, what a lift, what a jerk!"
Jimmy McGee on weightlifting in the Olympic Games

" ...and so they have not been able to improve their 100 per cent record."
BBC Sports Round-up

" 3–0 Finland and Russia are lucky to get nothing."
No credit for the Russians from the BBC's ice hockey commentator

" If our swimmers want to win any more medals,
they'll have to put their skates on. "
Does Dave Brenner want swimming on ice?

" Ralph, I would like to be able to tell the folks
what happened on that play, but the Florida
cheerleaders were shaking their fuzzy things right
in front of us. "
**University of Kentucky commentator Cawood
Ledford clearly gets distracted by pom poms**

I'm not a big Gay guy.
**Pundit Rick Majerus was stating his player,
rather than sexual, preference about college
player Rudy Gay**

" Don't buy upgrades, ride up grades. "
Eddy Merckx

" Crashing is part of cycling as crying is part of love."
Johan Museeuw

" As long as I breathe, I attack."
Bernard Hinault

I learned how fast you can go from being an international hero to being a reference in a joke on a late night talk show.
Michael Phelps

" I feel most at home in the water. I disappear. That's where I belong."
Michael Phelps

" I thought lacrosse was what you find in la church."
Actor/comedian Robin Williams

" Endless motorbike talk can, and does, bore me. "
World motorbike champion, Barry Sheene

That's the closest I'll ever come to knowing what it's like to have a baby. It was just torture.
Sir Bradley Wiggins on the UCI Hour Record

" That was like throwing three pickled onions into a thimble! "
Sid Waddell, darts commentator

" If everything seems under control, you're just not going fast enough. "
Mario Andretti

" I would have probably stolen cars – it would have given me the same adrenaline rush as racing. "
Valentino Rossi, Moto GP rider

Other Sports

" It's the iron in the mind, not in the supplements, that wins medals. "
Sir Steve Redgrave

" Swimming isn't everything, winning is. "
Mark Spitz, US swimmer

They've made me angry and you don't want to make me angry.
Sailor Ben Ainslie warns his opponents at the 2012 Olympics

" Blood, sweat and respect. First two you give. Last you earn. Give it. Earn it. "
Dwayne 'The Rock' Johnson

Romanians have a saying, "Not every dog has a bagel on its tail." It means that not all the streets are paved with gold. When I began my career, I just wanted to do cartwheels.
Nadia Comaneci, gymnast

" I don't know. I've never won the America's Cup. But I can tell you this: it certainly isn't worth 100 million dollars to lose the America's Cup. "
Investor Larry Ellison's response when asked whether his $100 million investment was worth it

" That's like giving Dracula the keys to the blood bank. "
Sid Waddell

Other Sports

" The touching of gloves may be the only punch
Fujita lands."
**MMA commentator Stephen Quadros didn't think
much of Kazuyuki Fujita's chances**

" Mark Lee's long arms reaching up like
giant testicles."
**Aussie Rules great Jack Dyer confuses parts of the
anatomy when trying to describe an
octopus's tentacles**

" If we'd had Phil Taylor at Hastings against the
Normans, they'd have gone home."
**Sid Waddell thinks a lot of Phil Taylor's
darting prowess**